Graded Go Problems for Beginners

Volume One
Introductory Problems

by
Kano Yoshinori 9-dan

translated and edited by
Richard Bozulich

Kiseido Publishing Company
Chigasaki, Los Angeles, Amsterdam

Published by
Kiseido Publishing Company
Kagawa 4-48-32, Chigasaki
Kanagawa, Japan 253-0082

ISBN 978-4-906574-46-9

First printing August 1987
Revised Edition September 2016

Contents

About the Author and Translator

Kano Yoshinori was born on April 14, 1928 in Kyoto and died on May 2, 1999. He came to Tokyo at the age of nine and became a disciple of Suzuki Hideko 5-dan. He became 1-dan in 1943 and in 1968 he attained the top rank of 9-dan. In 1948 he won the Young Professional's Championship, in 1955 he won the top section of the Oteai, and in 1961 he won the 5th Prime Minister's Cup. He played in the 14th, 20th, 25th, and 26th Honinbo leagues. In 1975 he went to Austria and Russia, then in 1979 he led a team of high school go players to China for a goodwill match. He graduated from the Japanese Literature Department of Japan University, making him one of the few professional go players to have graduated from university. His most prominent disciple is the Taiwanese go player, O Rissei 9-dan, winner of the 2000, 2002, and 2001 Kisei titles. In 2001 he won the Judan title.

Richard Bozulich is the president of Kiseido Publishing Company. He learned how to play go in 1958 while a studying mathematics at the University of California, Berkeley. He came to Japan in 1967 to study go and founded The Ishi Press for the purpose of publishing go books in English. In 1982, he founded Kiseido.

Preface

This is the first volume of a four-volume collection of problems and is intended for players who are learning the rules of go. The nearly 1500 problems this set contains cover all phases of the game, from the opening to the endgame.

It is assumed that the reader is studying a good and comprehensive beginner's book on go, such as *Go: A Complete Introduction to the Game* by Cho Chikun. For reference, however, we have included a brief summary of the rules.

It is my hope that by studying and solving the problems in these four volumes, the reader will establish a solid foundation on which to build his future progress.

Kano Yoshinori 9-dan
March, 1985

How To Play Go

Go is usually played on a 19x19 grid, or board, as it is usually referred to, resulting in 361 intersections on which the pieces, or stones as they are usually called, are placed. *Dia. 1* shows the empty board. Note the nine marked points on the board. These points are referred to as the 'star points'. They serve as points of reference, as well as markers on which stones are placed in handicap games.

Although most go games are played on a 19x19 board, beginners often learn the game on a 9x9 board with 81 intersections. After a few games they will move up to a 13x13 board, then graduate to the standard 19x19 board.

A standard go set contains 361 stones: 181 black stones and 180 white. They are put inside containers, called bowls.

To play go, it is necessary to learn only a few simple rules. We will first start with seven general rules.

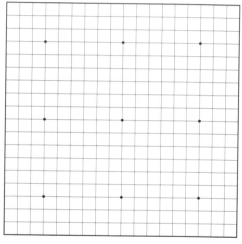

Dia. 1

General Rules

1. Go is played between two people.
2. One side plays with the black stones, the other side with the white ones. The players take turns playing their moves, one at a time.
3. A move consists of placing a stone on an intersection of the board. Stones can also be placed on the edge and corner points.
4. Once a stone is placed on an intersection, it cannot be moved to another point.
5. When there is a difference in strength between the contestants, the weaker player places extra stones on the board to compensate for the difference in strength.
6. In an even game, the side holding the black stones always plays first, but in a handicap game, it is White who plays first.
7. The object of the game is to take and control more territory than your opponent.

An Example Game

To show how the game of go is played and its objective achieved, we present a game on a 9x9 board. Don't think so much about the reasons for the moves, rather, concentrate on how Black and White form territory.

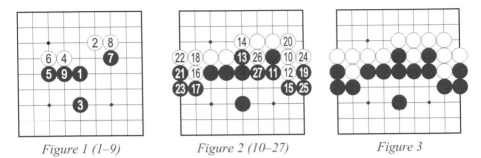

Figure 1 (1–9)   Figure 2 (10–27)   Figure 3

Figure 1 (1–9). Black plays his first move on the central point and White plays 2. With the moves to Black 9, White has staked out the top as his territory and Black has laid claim to the bottom.

Figure 2 (10–27). White 10 and 12 reduce the size of Black's territory at the bottom. Before blocking at 15, Black plays 13, threatening to break into White's territory at the top. White must defend with 14. White again expands his territory with 16 and 18, while reducing Black's. Black 19 forces White to connect at 20. After Black plays 27, the boundaries of Black's and White's territories have been defined and the game is over.

Figure 3 shows the result. White has taken control of 23 intersections and Black 31. Therefore, Black wins by 8 points.

Four Technical Rules

1. Capturing Stones

A stone can be captured if all the lines leading out to adjacent intersections are blocked by the opponent's stones. In *Dia. 2*, if Black plays 1 in any of these three positions, the white stone will be captured and taken off the board. The stone that is threatened with capture is said to be in 'atari'.

This rule also applies to groups of two or more stones. For example, Black can capture three stones and take them

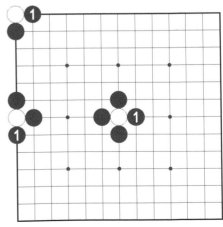

Dia. 2

off the board in the lower right of *Dia. 3* by playing at 1. Black 1 in the upper left also captures four stones.

In the previous example game, no captures were made, but there were a few threats to capture. For example, when Black played 17 in Figure 2, White defended with 18. If White had ignored Black 17 (the marked stone in *Dia. 4*), Black could atari the marked white stone with 1 in *Dia. 4*. White could also atari with 2, but Black would capture with 3.

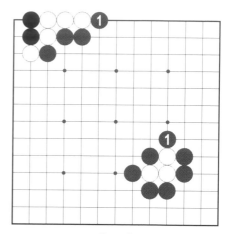

Dia. 3

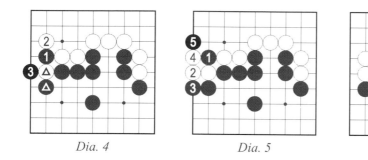

| *Dia. 4* | *Dia. 5* | *Dia. 6* |

Suppose White tries to escape capture by extending to 2 in *Dia. 5*. Black pursues him by making another atari with 3. White continues his attempt to escape by crawling to 4. Even though this move ataries the stone at 1, White has not gotten out of atari himself and Black captures three stones with 5.

Now look at Black 19 in Figure 2 (the marked stone in *Dia. 6*). We said that this move forces White to defend at 20. What happens if he doesn't? Black will atari two stones with 1 in *Dia. 6*. There is no way to escape, so White must atari with 2 and Black captures two stones with 3.

What about White 22 and 24 in Figure 2? Both these moves are atari and Black defends against capture by connecting at 23 and 25 respectively.

You should note that defending against an atari is not mandatory. There are many positions in which the best move is not to defend.

2. Suicide Is Illegal

Although a player can make a move anywhere he chooses, there are two restrictions. The first one is the prohibition against suicide. In the four positions shown in *Dia. 7*, The moves White 1 are illegal. That is, White is not allowed to play on these points because he places his stone(s) in atari and they will be taken off the board. However, you should note that there is no restriction on Black with respect to playing on these points.

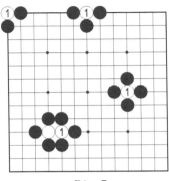

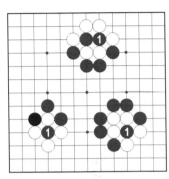

Dia. 7	*Dia. 8*

The moves Black 1 in *Dia. 8* may seem illegal, like the ones in Dia. 7, but even though Black seems to be playing on prohibited points, he is capturing stones, so these moves are not illegal. In other words, capturing stones takes priority over illegal moves.

3. Ko

Look at the position in *Dia. 9* where Black captures a stone with 1. The result is shown in *Dia. 10*. You might think that White could recapture with 1 in *Dia. 11*, but the position in *Dia. 12* is the same as *Dia. 9* before Black captured with 1.

If Black were allowed to recapture again, an endless repetition of capture-recapture could result if both sides refuse to stop. This kind of situation is called a ko.

Dia. 9	*Dia. 10*	*Dia. 11*	*Dia. 12*

To prevent this from happening, the following special rule was created:

If one side captures a stone in a ko,

the other side cannot recapture on the next move.

Another and more elegant way this rule is stated is:

No move is allowed that will recreate a previous board position.

The next example on a 13x13 board shows how a ko can arise in a game.

Figure 4 (1–14). Black stakes out the top with 1 and 3, while White plays 2 and 4 at the bottom. The game continues to Black 13, after which White captures the stone at 7 with 14, starting a ko.

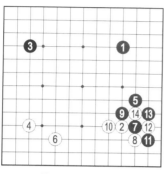

Figure 4 (1–14)

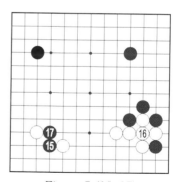

Figure 5 (15–17)

Figure 5 (15–17). Because of the ko rule, Black cannot immediately capture the stone at 14. Therefore, he plays elsewhere at 15, threatening to split White's stones on the lower left in two. If White defends with 16, Black can capture the ko with 17.

Figure 6 (18–20). It is now White's turn to make a ko threat. He attaches at 18. Black captures a stone with 19, ending the ko, but White takes the initiative at the top with 20.

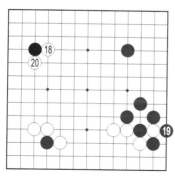

Figure 6 (18–20)

Figure 7 (15–17)

Figure 7 (15–17). Instead of 16 in Figure 5, White might choose to end the ko by connecting with 16. In that case, Black would split the white stones on the left in two with 17. Regardless of the strategic merits of these moves, this game shows how a ko is fought.

4. The End of the Game

The game is over when there are no longer any profitable points to be taken. This stage has been reached in *Dia. 13*. Four things must now be done.

A. Both sides must first agree that the game is over.

B. The neutral points are filled and the defects in one's territory are defended.

C. The dead stones are removed from the board and placed in the opponent's territory.

D. The amount of territory each side has is counted.

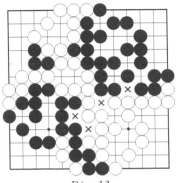
Dia. 13

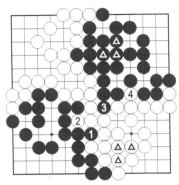
Dia. 14

In *Dia. 13*, the points marked with an 'x' are the neutral points. Since they have no value, it doesn't matter which side plays on them, but it is customary for the players to take turns filling them as is done in *Dia. 14*. Neither side has any defects, so defensive moves are not necessary.

There are three dead white stones and three dead black ones. These stones have no chance to make two eyes, so they are removed from the board. White removes the three black stones in the upper left in *Dia. 13* and places them in Black's territory in the upper right in *Dia. 14* (the three marked black stones). For his part, Black removes the three white stones in the lower left in *Dia. 13* and places them in White's territory in the lower right in *Dia. 14* (the three marked white stones). The territory is now counted.

Black has 20 points in the lower left and 19 points in the upper right for a total of 39 points.

White has 16 points in the lower right and 22 points in the upper left for a total of 38 points.

Black wins by one point.

This is all you need to know to start playing go.

Living Groups

Are there stones that are completely surrounded but still alive? If you understand the rule about suicide, you should be able to answer this question.

In *Dia. 1*, there are three black groups which can never be captured. In the group at the bottom, White can never play on the points A or B because he would be committing suicide. Therefore, even if all the outside liberties Black's outside liberties are filled, Black can never be captured. For the same reason, the black group in the upper left corner and the one on the right side are also immune from capture.

The points A and B in *Dia. 1* are called eyes. If a group has eyes in at least two separated places, the group is said to be 'alive'. It doesn't matter where these eyes are: in the center, on the edge, or in the corner.

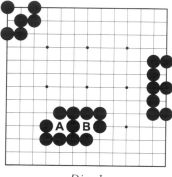

Dia. 1

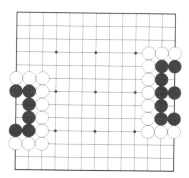

Dia. 2

As we explained above, it is impossible for the black group on the right in *Dia. 2* to be captured, even though it is completely surrounded. But the black group on the left is dead; that is, White can capture it by playing 1 in *Dia. 3*.

If Black captures at 2, he is left with one liberty. White plays back in at 1 and captures the black stones. You might have thought that Black had two eyes, but this is just a two-space eye and not two separated eyes like the group on the right.

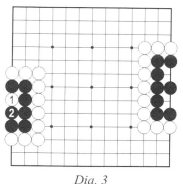

Dia. 3

False Eyes

The black stones at the bottom in *Dia. 4* are dead since they have only one real eye. They certainly have a two-space eye in the corner, which is one real eye, but the eye at A, even though it looks like an eye, is a 'false eye'. If White fills the two liberties of the three-stone group surrounding the point A, Black will be in atari and will have to defend by connecting at A. Black's only eye is the two-point eye space in the corner.

In the group at the top, the points A and B on the edge are also false eyes. Black can be forced to play on these points, so his group will be left with only one eye, so it is dead.

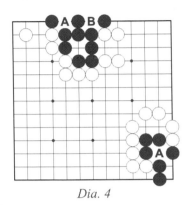

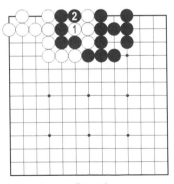

Dia. 4   *Dia. 5*

Seki

Look at the position in *Dia. 5*. The group of four black stones and the group of three white stones in the middle do not have eyes. However, both groups are alive since neither side can atari the other.

For example, if White attacks the black stones by playing at 1 in *Dia. 6*, he puts himself into atari and Black will capture four white stones with 2. On the other hand, if Black plays at 1, White will capture five black stones by playing at 2. As you can see, neither side can play here without suffering a loss, so the stones remain on the board at the end of the game. This kind of a position is called a seki.

A necessary condition for a seki to exist is that all the stones surrounding the stones in a seki are alive.

The two points between the groups in seki do not count as territory.

Dia. 6

In the seki in *Dia. 7*, each of the black and white groups have an eye, but there is a white stone inside Black's eye. At the end of the game, before Black passes, he will capture this stone, thereby gaining a point. However, the eye in each of the groups in the seki are not counted as territory.

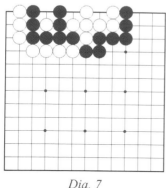

Dia. 7

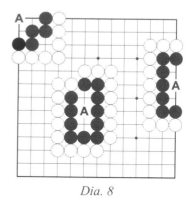

Dia. 8

Nakade

It often happens that when a group of stones is surrounded and has an eye space, your opponent will place a stone inside that eye space, and reduce it to one eye. This kind of move is called *nakade*.

The three positions (in the corner, in the center, and on the side) in *Dia. 8* are examples of a three-space eye: White can kill each of these groups by playing on the point A. Such moves are examples of *nakade*. On the other hand, Black can make two eyes and live in each of these three positions by playing at A.

There are many varieties of eye spaces. They come in all sizes and shapes. Many of them can be reduced to one eye with nakade moves, others can not. You will find many examples in the problem section.You can find a complete discussion of this topic in Kiseido's publication ***The Basics of Life and Death*** (see page 190)

Handicaps

When there is a difference in strength between two players, the weaker player will take a handicap and place stones on specified points to compensate for the difference. Handicaps range from nine stones to two stones.

Dia. 9 (next page) shows the order of placement for a nine-stone handicap. In an eight-stone handicap, Black doesn't put the stone at 9. For a seven-stone handicap, Black 7 is placed on the central point. Finally, for a six-stone handicap, Black only places the stones from 1 to 6.

The placements for five- to two-stone handicaps are shown in *Dia. 10*.

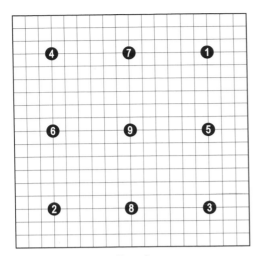

Dia. 9

Komi

Since Black moves first, he has the advantage. In order to make a game an even contest, Black concedes to White a number of points of territory before the start of the game. When the score is counted, these points are subtracted from Black's score. This compensation is called *komi*. The usual komi given to White by Black is 6½ points. Although half points do not arise in actual play, it is a device used in tournament games to ensure that draws do not occur.

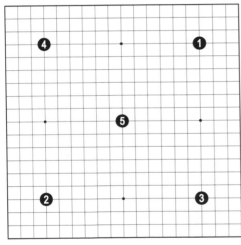

Dia. 10

Other Books to Continue Your Study of Go

This has been a brief introduction to go. It is recommended that you study a more complete presentation of the rules. The book we recommend is *Go: A Complete Introduction to the Game, by Cho Chikun*, which is available from Kiseido Publishing Company (see page 188). Kiseido publishes a wide range of books, covering every aspect of the game. For a list of go books published by Kiseido, see *Go Books from Kiseido* at the end of this book (pages 188 to 191).

A Brief Glossary of Go Terms and Concepts

Aji — The possibilities that exists in a position. Although these possibilities may never be realized, their existence influences the course of the game and enables certain moves to be made.

Atari — When all the intersections except one directly adjacent to a stone or a group of stones are occupied by the opponent, the stone or group is said to be in 'atari'.

Dame — Neutral points which profit neither Black or White.

Dan — A ranking scale running from shodan (1-dan) up to 9-dan.

Double atari — Making an atari on two different groups of the same color.

Eye — A point which is surrounded by stones of the same color.

Gote — A move that your opponent can ignore. A gote move is usually defensive, so it will pose little or no threat to your opponent.

Hane — A hane is a diagonal move that bends (literally 'springs') around an opposing stone.

Ko — A shape in which your stone is captured, but it is illegal to recapture on the next move.

Kyu — An amateur ranking scale running from about 30-kyu (a complete beginner) up to 1-kyu, the highest rank before shodan.

Miai — Points in a position that are of equal value. If one player occupies one of them, the other player will usually take the other.

Moyo — A large framework of potential territory.

Nakade — A move that plays into a large eye space with the aim of reducing it to a single eye.

Ponnuki — The shape left when a stone is captured by four opposing stones.

Oi-otoshi — A move that ataries a group so that no matter how it is defended, the group will still be in atari.

Oshi-tsubushi — A shape in which you atari two or more of your opponent's stones so that any defense of them would be an illegal move.

Seki — Dual life. A situation in which neither of two groups of opposing stones has two eyes, but neither side can attack the other without losing his stones.

Sente — A move that your opponent cannot ignore, otherwise he will suffer an unacceptable loss.

Snapback — A tactic in which one stone is offered as a sacrifice and, if it is taken, the capturing stones can then be captured.

Shodan — 1-dan. The lowest dan ranking. The first level of an expert player.

Tesuji — A skillful tactical move. A brilliancy.

Part One

Problems

Introductory Problems
Level One

Section 1. How to Capture Stones

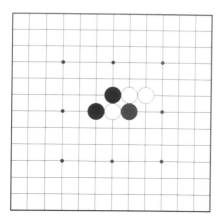

Problem 1. Black to play.
How can Black capture a white stone?

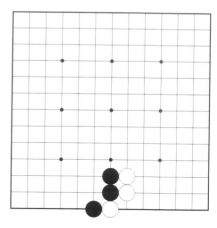

Problem 2. Black to play.
How can Black capture a white stone?

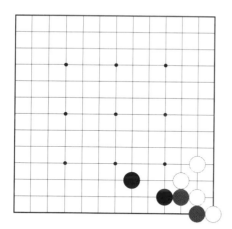

Problem 3. Black to play.
How can Black capture a white stone?

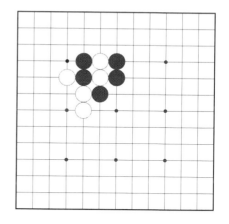

Problem 4. Black to play.
How can Black capture two white stones?

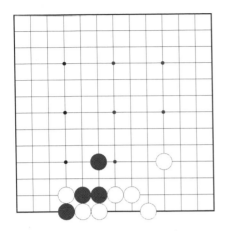

Problem 5. Black to play.
How can Black capture two white stones?

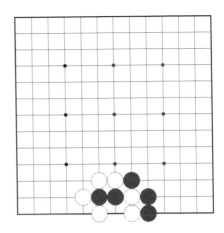

Problem 6. Black to play.
How can Black capture two white stones?

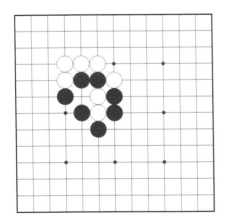

Problem 7. Black to play.
How can Black capture two white stones?

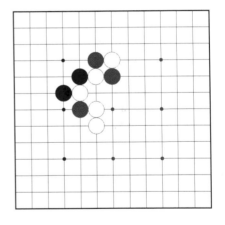

Problem 8. Black to play.
How can Black capture two white stones?

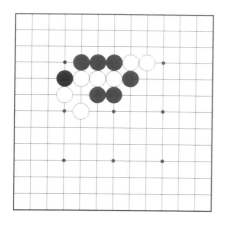

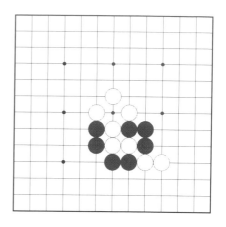

Problem 9. Black to play.

How can Black capture three white stones?

Problem 10. Black to play.

How can Black capture three white stones?

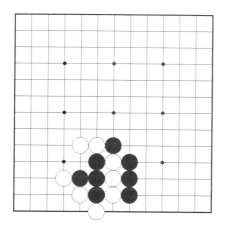

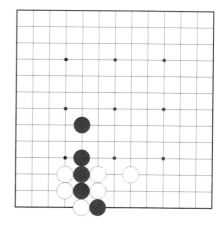

Problem 11. Black to play.

How can Black capture three white stones?

Problem 12. Black to play.

How can Black capture a white stone?

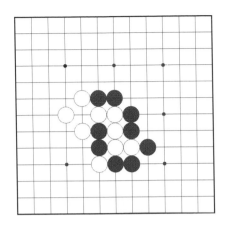

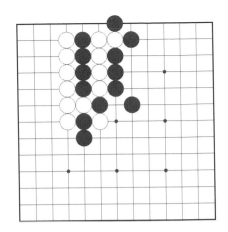

Problem 13. Black to play.
How can Black capture some white stones?

Problem 14. Black to play.
How can Black capture some white stones?

Section 2. How to Rescue Endangered Stones

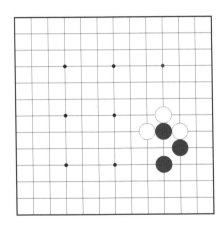

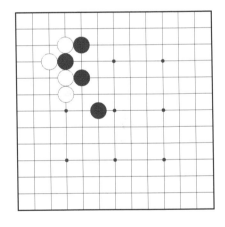

Problem 15. Black to play.
How can Black rescue in his stone in atari?

Problem 16. Black to play.
One black stone is about to be captured. How can Black rescue it?

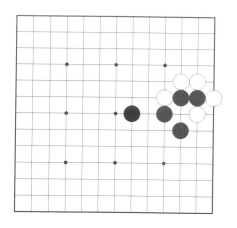

Problem 17. Black to play.

Two black stones are in danger of being captured. How can Black rescue them?

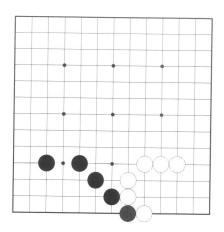

Problem 18. Black to play.

One black stone is about to be captured. How can Black rescue it?

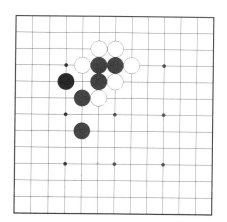

Problem 19. Black to play.

Three black stones are in danger of being captured. How can Black rescue them?

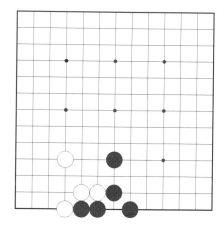

Problem 20. Black to play.

Black doesn't want to lose his two stones in atari. How can he rescue them?

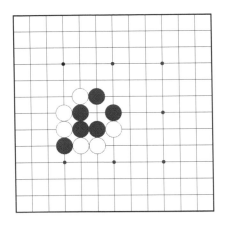

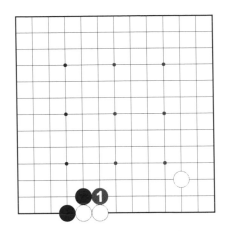

Problem 21. Black to play.

How can Black play to rescue his three endangered stones?

Problem 22. White to play.

Black has ataried with 1. Is there a way for White to rescue his two stones?

Section 3. Recognizing Atari

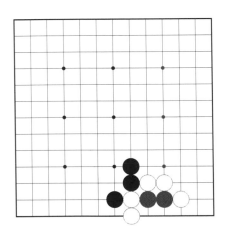

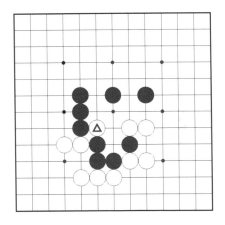

Problem 23. Black to play.

How should Black atari the two white stones on the edge?

Problem 24. Black to play.

In which direction should Black atari the marked stone?

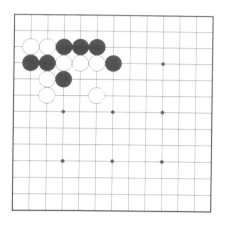

Problem 25. Black to play.

How should Black atari the three white stones?

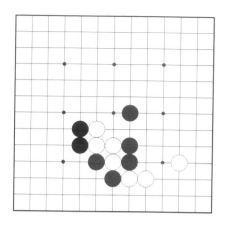

Problem 26. Black to play.

How should Black atari the four white stones?

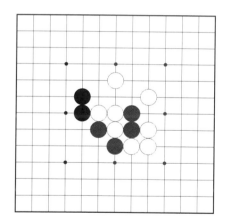

Problem 27. Black to play.

How should Black atari the three white stones?

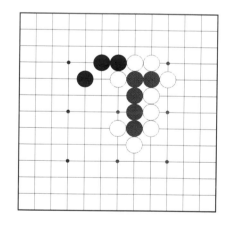

Problem 28. Black to play.

How should Black atari the lone white stone?

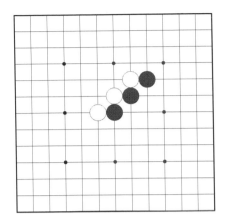

Problem 29. Black to play.
How can Black atari two stones at the same time?

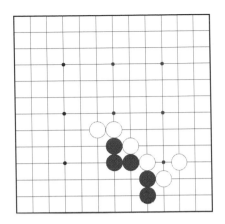

Problem 30. Black to play.
How can Black atari two stones at the same time?

Section 4. Separating and Linking up Stones

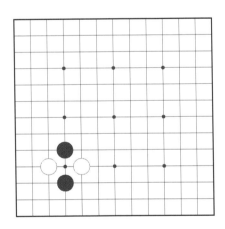

Problem 31. Black to play.
How can Black link up his stones?

Problem 32. Black to play.
How Black link up his stones?

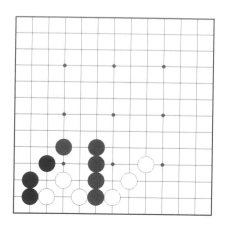

Problem 33. Black to play.

How can Black prevent the white stones from linking up?

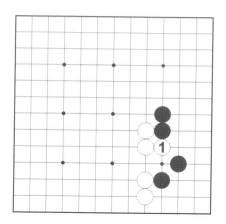

Problem 34. Black to play.

How should Black respond to White 1?

Section 5. Ko

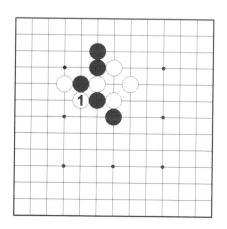

Problem 35. Black to play.

How should Black answer the double atari of White 1?

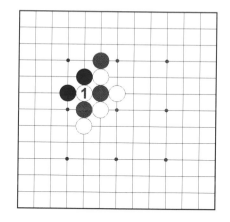

Problem 36. Black to play.

White 1 captures a black stone in a ko. How should Black respond?

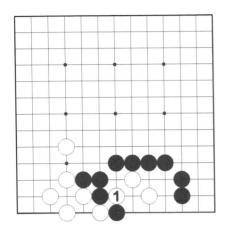

Problem 37. Black to play.

How should Black respond to White 1?

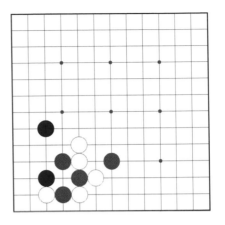

Problem 38. Black to play.

What is Black's best move?

Section 6. Ladders

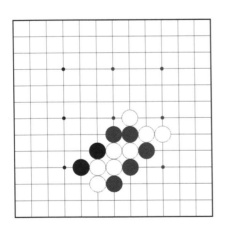

Problem 39. Black to play.

How can Black capture five stones?

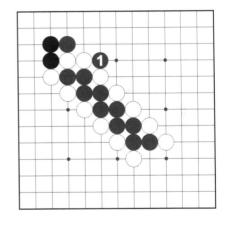

Problem 40. White to play.

Black plays a double atari with 1. How should White respond?

Section 7. Life and Death

(A group of stones is alive if it can make two 'eyes'. Such stones can never be captured. A group is dead if it cannot make two eyes. Such stones will be taken off the board as prisoners at the end of the game.)

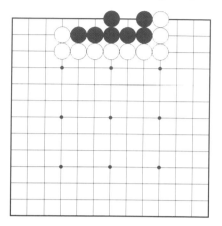

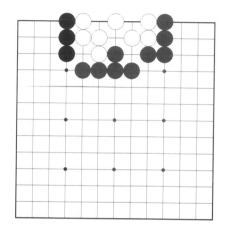

Problem 41. Black to play.

How can Black make two eyes for his seven stones?

Problem 42. Black to play.

Where should Black play to kill the white stones?

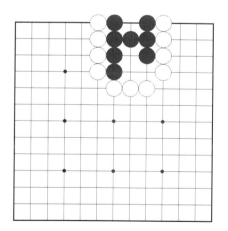

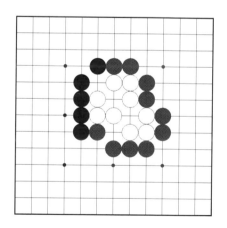

Problem 43. Black to play.

How can Black make two eyes for his seven-stone group?

Problem 44. Black to play.

How can Black kill all of the white stones?

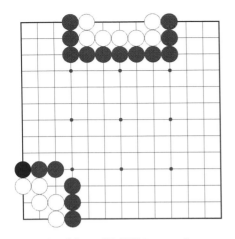

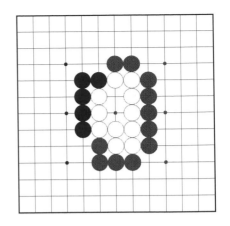

Problem 45. White to play.
How can White make two eyes for his groups at the top and at the bottom?

Problem 46. Alive or dead?
White is surrounding two empty points. Is his group alive of dead?

Section 8. How to Play in the Opening

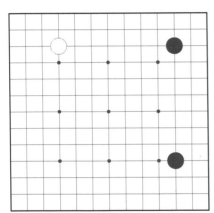

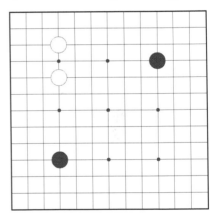

Problem 47. White to play.
Where should White play?

(There is more than one correct answer.)

Problem 48. Black to play.
Where should Black play?

(There is more than one correct answer.)

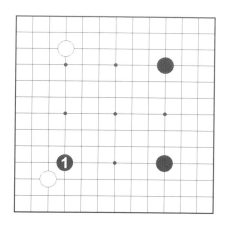

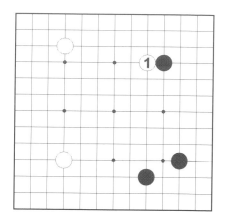

Problem 49. White to play.

How should White answer the shoulder hit of Black 1?

Problem 50. Black to play.

White 1 is a bad move. How should Black respond?

Section 9. The Endgame and Other Moves

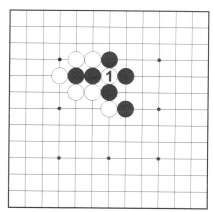

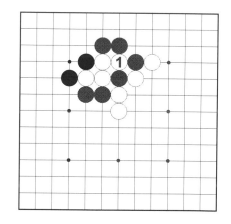

Problem 51. Black to play.

How should Black play after White captures two stones with 1?

Problem 52. Black to play.

How should Black play after White captures a stone with 1?

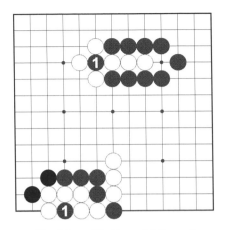

Problem 53. Legal Moves?
In the positions at the top and bottom, is it a legal move for Black to play 1?

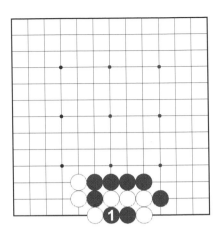

Problem 54. Legal Move?
Is it a legal move for Black to play 1?

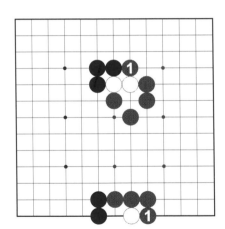

Problem 55. Remove from the board?
In the positions at the top and bottom, can Black remove the white stones from the board after he plays 1?

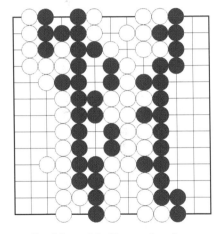

Problem 56. Neutral points.
The game is over, but there are two neutral points to be played before counting can begin. Where are they?

(Neutral points are points that profit neither Black nor White. It doesn't matter which side plays on them. *Dame* in Japanese.)

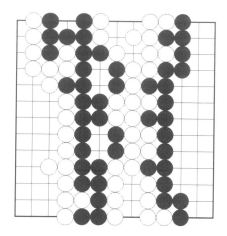

Problem 57. Calculate the territories.

No stones have been captured. Who wins and by how many points?

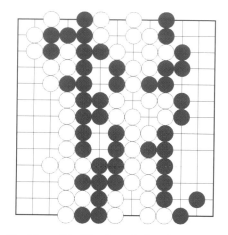

Problem 58. The last defensive moves.

Black and White have to play defensive moves inside their own territories before the last neutral points can be played. Where are these moves?

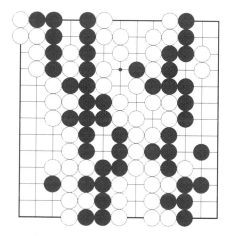

Problem 59. Remove from the board?

There are five dead white stones inside Black's territory and two dead black stones inside White's territory. Where are these stones?

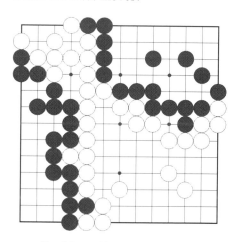

Problem 60. Black to play.

Where is the last point of profit?

Introductory Problems
Level Two

Section 1. How to Capture Stones

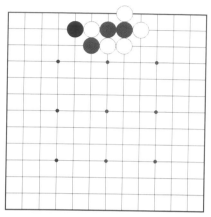

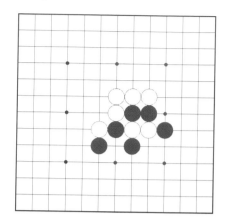

Problem 61. Black to play.

How can Black capture a stone and rescue his two stones in atari?

Problem 62. Black to play.

How can Black capture two white stones?

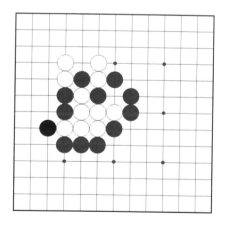

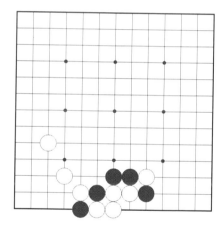

Problem 63. White to play.

There are two black stones in atari. Which one should White capture?

Problem 64. Black to play.

How can Black capture some white stones?

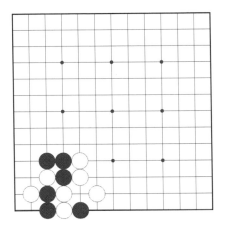

Problem 65. Black to play.

Black has two ways to capture? Which stone or stones should he take?

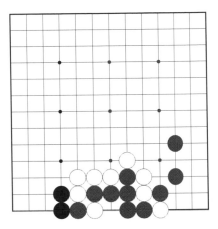

Problem 66. Black to play.

Which white stone should Black capture?

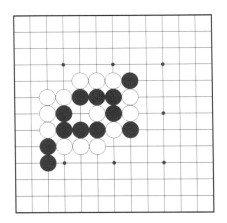

Problem 67. Black to play.

Which white stone should Black capture?

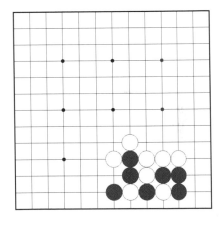

Problem 68. Black to play.

Which white stone should Black capture?

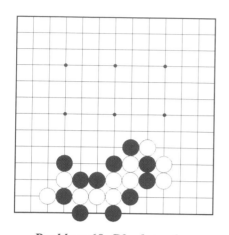

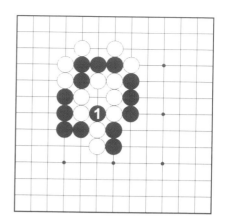

Problem 69. Black to play.
Which stone or stones should Black capture?

Problem 70. White to play.
Which stone or stones should White capture?

Section 2. How to Rescue Endangered Stones

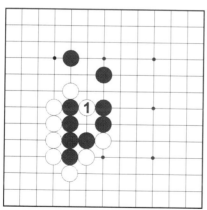

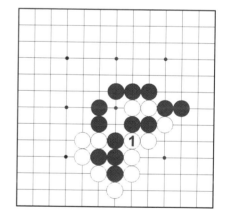

Problem 71. Black to play.
How should Black answer White 1?

Problem 72. Black to play.
How should Black answer White 1?

Section 3. How to Atari

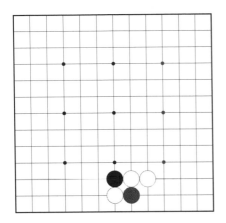

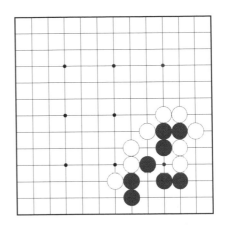

Problem 73. Black to play.

Black has two ways to atari the lone white stone. Which one is best?

Problem 74. White to play.

Which is the best way for White to atari three stones?

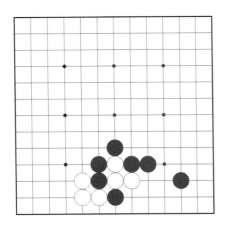

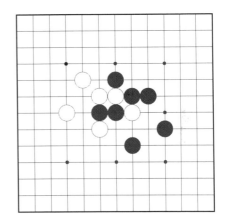

Problem 75. Black to play.

How should Black atari the three white stones?

Problem 76. White to play.

How should White atari the two black stones?

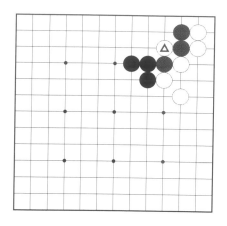

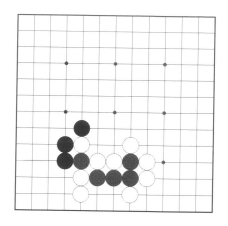

Problem 77. Black to play.
Black has two ways to atari the marked stone? Which one should he play?

Problem 78. Black to play.
How should Black atari the two white stones?

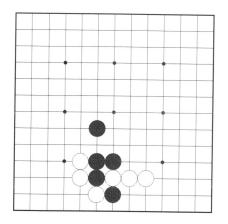

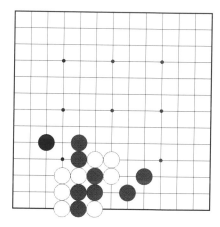

Problem 79. Black to play.
How should Black atari the white stone on the second line?

Problem 80. Black to play.
There is a white stone in atari. Should Black capture it?

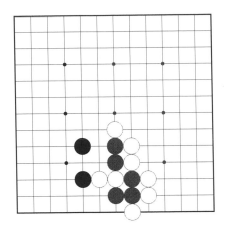

Problem 81. Black to play.

Which way should Black atari the two white stones?

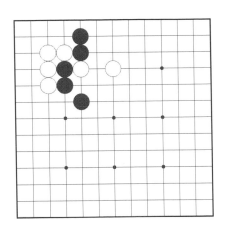

Problem 82. Black to play.

Which way should Black atari the lone white stone?

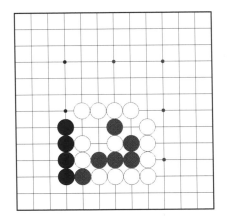

Problem 83. Black to play.

Which way should Black atari the two white stones?

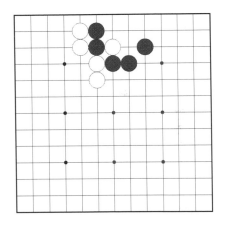

Problem 84. Black to play.

Which way should Black atari the lone white stone?

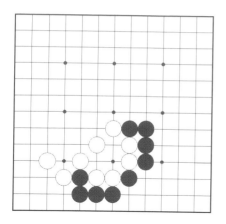

Problem 85. Black to play.

How can Black atari two groups at the same time (double atari)?

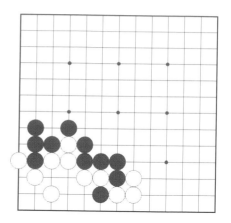

Problem 86. Black to play.

How can Black atari two groups at the same time?

Section 4. Ladders

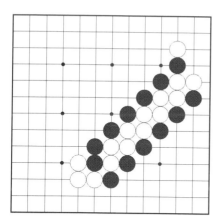

Problem 87. Black to play.

There are two ways that Black can atari White's eleven stones. Which way is best?

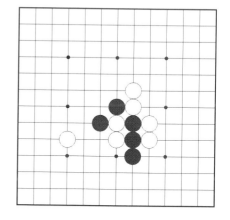

Problem 88. Black to play.

How should Black play so as to capture White's two stones in a ladder?

Section 5. Snapback and Related Moves

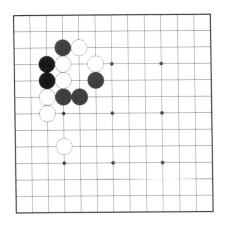

Problem 89. Black to play.

How should Black play so as to capture two stones?

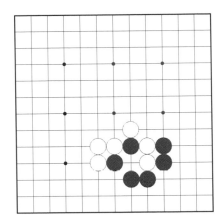

Problem 90. Black to play.

How should Black play so as to capture two stones?

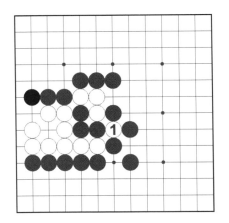

Problem 91. Black to play.

White captures three stones with 1. How should Black respond?

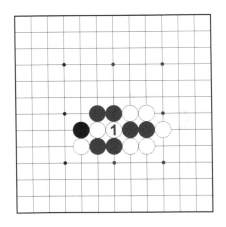

Problem 92. Black to play.

White captures two stones with 1. How should Black respond?

Section 6. Separating and Linking up Stones

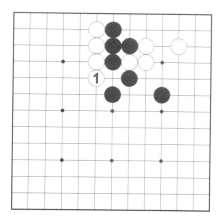

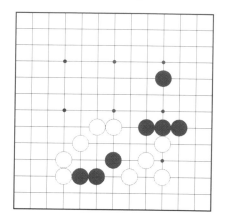

Problem 93. Black to play.
After White 1, how can Black link up his four stones at the top to the ones below?

Problem 94. Black to play.
How can Black link up all of his stones?

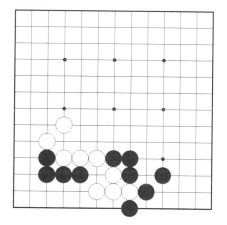

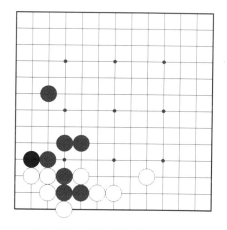

Problem 95. Black to play.
How can Black cut off the four white stones at the bottom from the ones above?

Problem 96. Black to play.
How can Black split White into two groups?

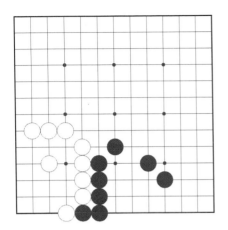

Problem 97. Black to play.

White has a defect in his position? How can Black take advantage of it?

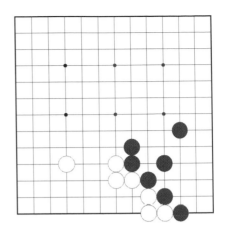

Problem 98. Black to play.

How should Black play in this position?

Section 7. Life and Death

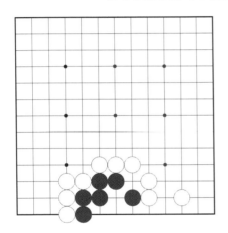

Problem 99. Black to play.

How can Black make two eyes and life for his group?

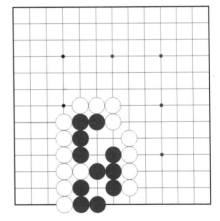

Problem 100. Black to play.

How can Black make two eyes and life for his group?

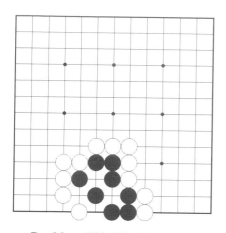

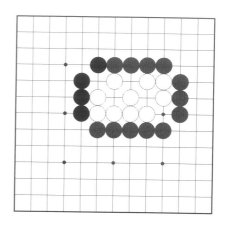

Problem 101. Black to play.

How can Black make two eyes and life for his group?

Problem 102. Black to play.

How can Black deprive the white group of two eyes, thereby killing it?

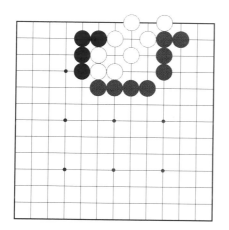

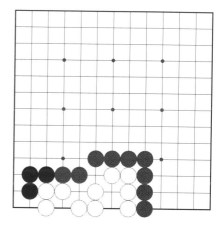

Problem 103. Black to play.

How can Black deprive the white group of two eyes, thereby killing it?

Problem 104. Black to play.

How can Black deprive the white group of two eyes, thereby killing it?

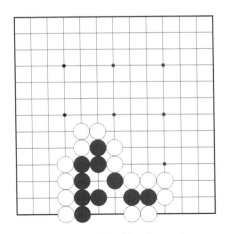

Problem 105. Black to play.

How can Black make two eyes and a living group?

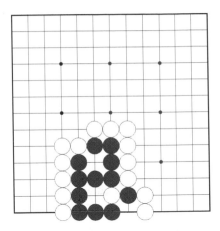

Problem 106. Black to play.

How can Black make two eyes and a living group?

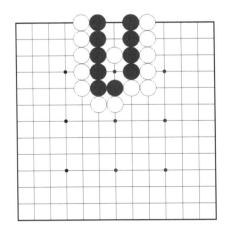

Problem 107. Black to play.

How can Black make two eyes and a living group?

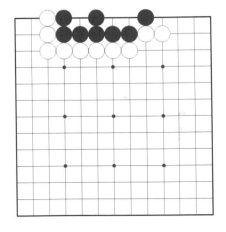

Problem 108. White to play.

How can White create a false eye and kill the black group?

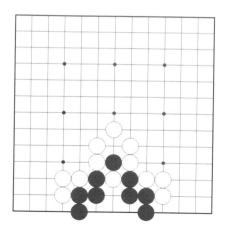

Problem 109. Black to play.

How can Black make two eyes and life for his group?

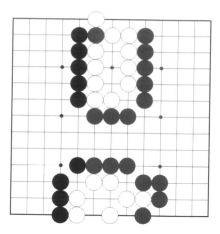

Problem 110. Black to play.

How can Black kill the white groups at the top and at the bottom?

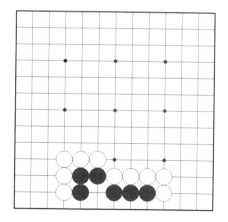

Problem 111. Black to play.

How can Black make two eyes and life for his group?

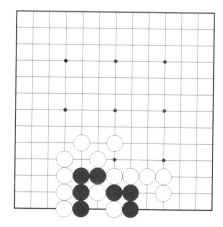

Problem 112. Alive or dead?

Is Black's group alive or dead? Is another Black move necessary?

Section 8. Ko

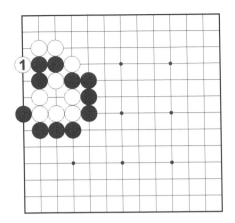

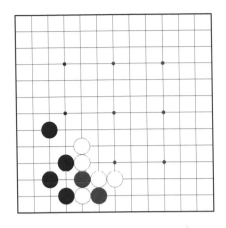

Problem 113. Black to play.
How should Black respond to White 1?

Problem 114. Black to play.
How should Black play in this position?

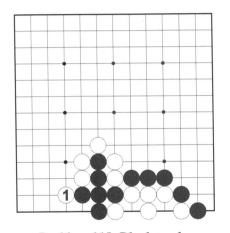

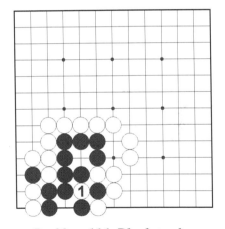

Problem 115. Black to play.
Black has just ataried with 1. How should Black answer?

Problem 116. Black to play.
White has just captured a stone in a ko. How should Black respond?

Section 9. How to Play in the Opening

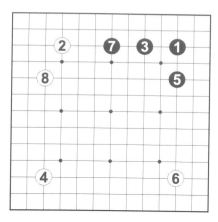

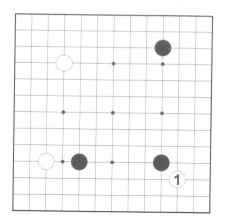

Problem 117.
Which side has the advantage?
After the moves to White 8, which side has the better game?

Problem 118. Black to play.
How should Black respond to White 1? (There are two correct answers.)

Section 10. The Endgame

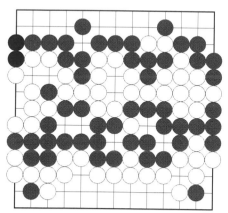

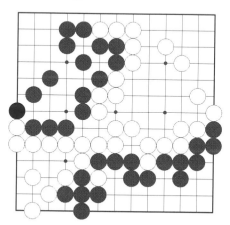

Problem 119. Determining the score.
The game is over. Both sides have three prisoners and both have three dead stones left on the board. Determine the score.

Problem 120. Black to play.
The game is almost over, but there are two profitable moves remaining. Where are they?

Introductory Problems
Level Three

Section 1. Making Life

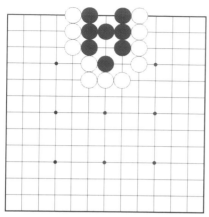

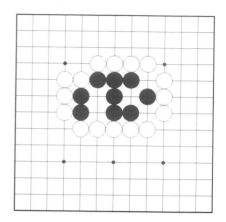

Problem 121. Black to play. (1 move)
How can Black make two eyes and life for his group?

Problem 122. Black to play. (1 move)
How can Black make two eyes and life for his group?

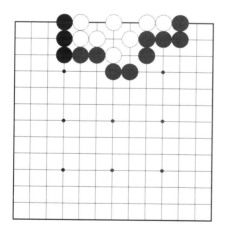

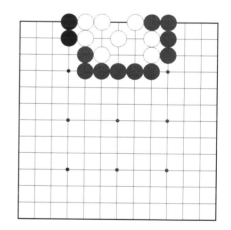

Problem 123. White to play. (1 move)
How can Black make two eyes and life for his group?

Problem 124. White to play. (1 move)
How can Black make two eyes and life for his group?

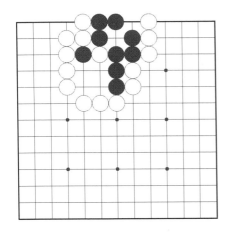

Problem 125. Black to play. (1 move)

How can Black make two eyes and life for his group?

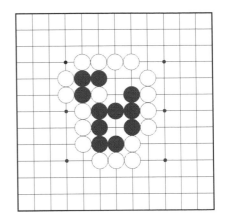

Problem 126. Black to play. (1 move)

How can Black make two eyes and life for his group?

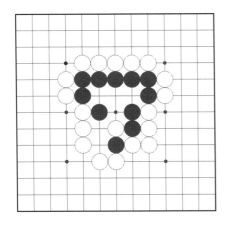

Problem 127. Black to play. (1 move)

How can Black make two eyes and life for his group?

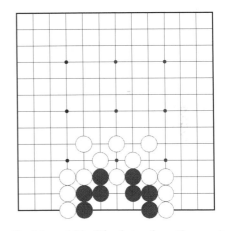

Problem 128. Black to play. (1 move)

How can Black make two eyes and life for his group?

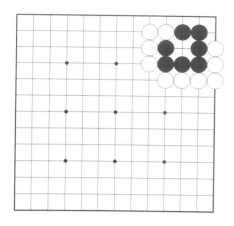

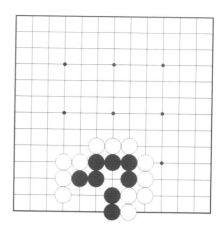

Problem 129. Black to play. (1 move)
How can Black make two eyes and life for his group?

Problem 130. Black to play. (1 move)
How can Black make two eyes and life for his group?

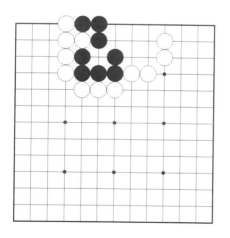

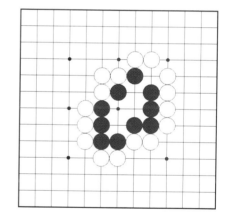

Problem 131. Black to play. (1 move)
How can Black make two eyes and life for his group?

Problem 132. Black to play. (1 move)
How can Black make two eyes and life for his group?

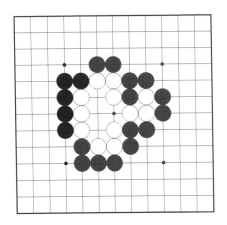

Problem 133. White to play. (1 move)
How can White make two eyes and life for his group?

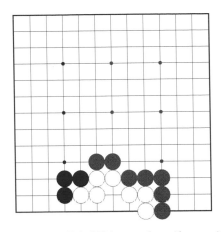

Problem 134. White to play. (1 move)
How can White make two eyes and life for his group?

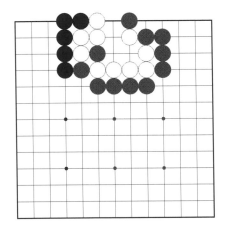

Problem 135. White to play. (1 move)
How can White make two eyes and life for his group?

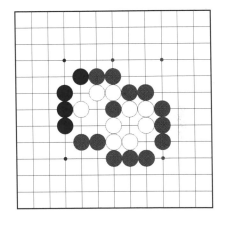

Problem 136. White to play. (1 move)
How can White make two eyes and life for his group?

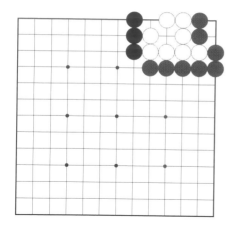

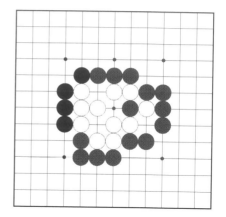

Problem 137. White to play. (1 move)

How can White make two eyes and life for his group?

Problem 138. White to play. (1 move)

How can White make two eyes and life for his group?

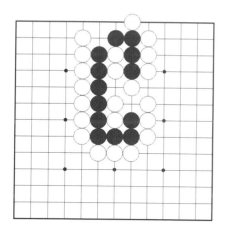

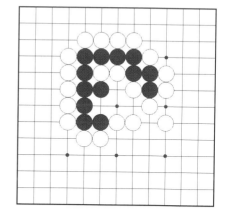

Problem 139. Black to play. (1 move)

How can Black make two eyes and life for his group?

Problem 140. Black to play. (1 move)

How can Black make two eyes and life for his group?

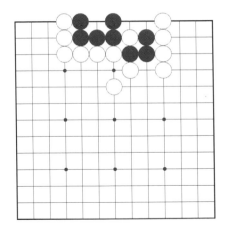

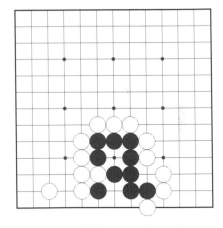

Problem 141. Black to play. (1 move)
How can Black make two eyes and life for his group?

Problem 142. Black to play. (1 move)
How can Black make two eyes and life for his group?

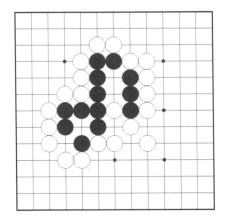

Problem 143. Black to play. (3 moves)
How can Black make two eyes and life for his group?

Problem 144. Black to play. (1 move)
How can Black make two eyes and life for his group?

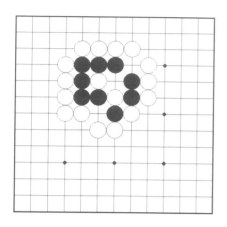

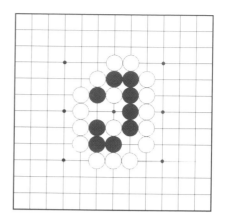

Problem 145. Black to play. (1 move)
How can Black make two eyes and life for his group?

Problem 146. Black to play. (1 move)
How can Black make two eyes and life for his group?

Section 2. Killing Groups

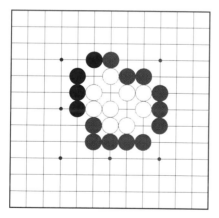

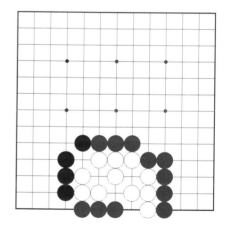

Problem 147. Black to play. (1 move)
How can Black kill the white group?

Problem 148. Black to play. (1 move)
How can Black kill the white group?

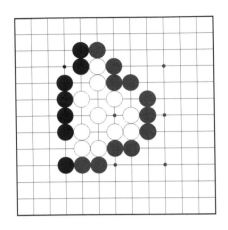

Problem 149. Black to play. (1 move)
How can Black kill the white group?

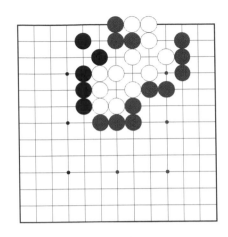

Problem 150. Black to play. (1 move)
How can Black kill the white group?

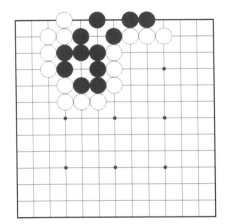

Problem 151. White to play. (1 move)
How can White kill the black group?

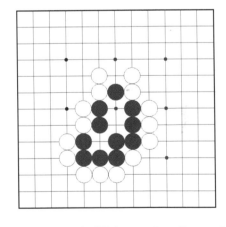

Problem 152. White to play. (1 move)
How can White kill the black group?

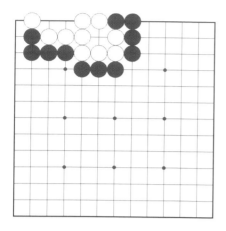

Problem 153. Black to play. (1 move)
How can Black kill the white group?

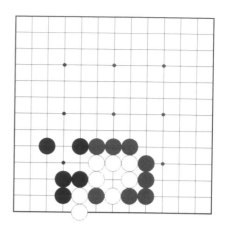

Problem 154. Black to play. (1 move)
How can Black kill the white group?

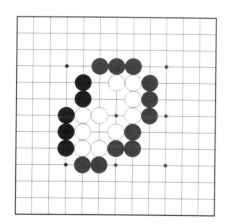

Problem 155. Black to play. (1 move)
How can Black kill the white group?

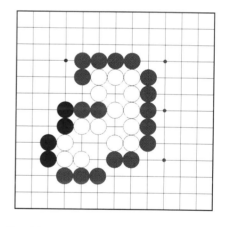

Problem 156. Black to play. (1 move)
How can Black kill the white group?

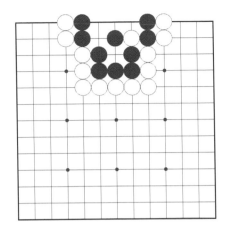

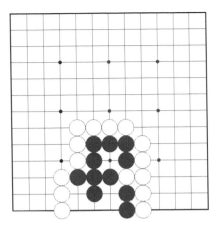

Problem 157. White to play. (1 move)
How can White kill the entire black group?

Problem 158. White to play. (1 move)
How can White kill the black group?

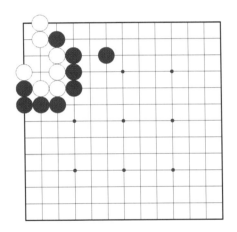

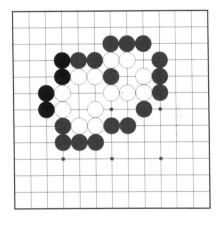

Problem 159. Black to play. (1 move)
How can Black kill the white group?

Problem 160. Black to play. (1 move)
How can Black kill the white group?

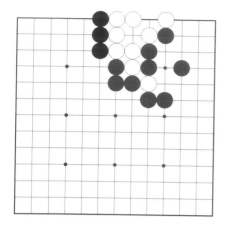

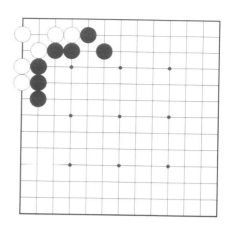

Problem 161. Black to play. (1 move)
How can Black kill the White group?

Problem 162. Black to play. (1 move)
How can Black kill the white group?

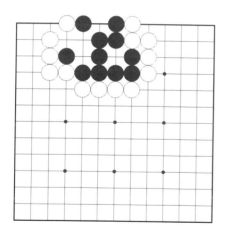

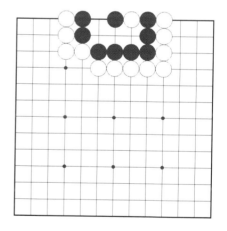

Problem 163. White to play. (1 move)
How can White kill the black group?

Problem 164. White to play. (1 move)
How can White kill the black group?

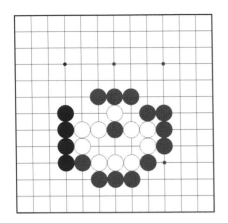

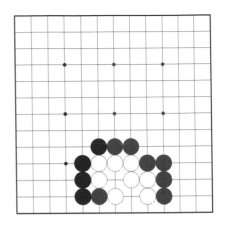

Problem 165. Black to play. (1 move)
How can Black kill the white group?

Problem 166. Black to play. (1 move)
How can Black kill the white group?

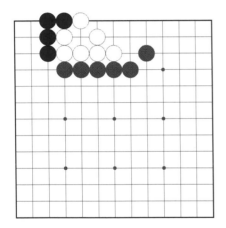

Problem 167. Black to play. (1 move)
How can Black kill the white group?

Section 3. Life and Death

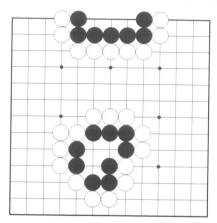

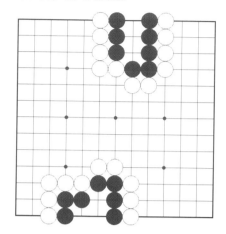

Problem 168.
Black and White to play. (1 move)

In the positions at the top and bottom, what is the result if Black plays first? If White plays first?

Problem 169.
Black and White to play. (1 move)

In the positions at the top and bottom, what is the result if Black plays first? If White plays first?

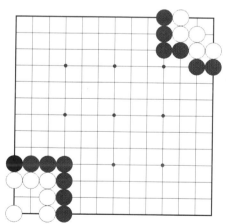

Problem 170.
Black and White to play. (1 move)

In the positions at the top and bottom, what is the result if Black plays first? If White plays first?

Section 4. Seki

(*Seki* — an impasse or stalemate position between two groups: if one side attacks, his stones will be captured.)

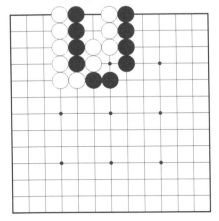

Problem 171. Black to play. (1 move)
How can Black create a seki?

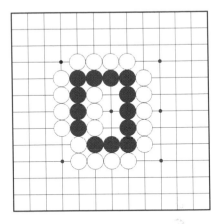

Problem 172. Black to play. (1 move)
How can Black live in a seki?

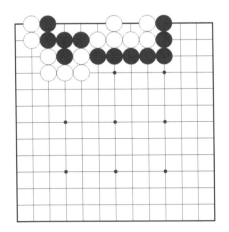

Problem 173. Black to play. (1 move)
How can Black live in a seki?

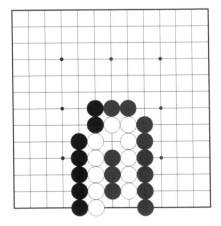

Problem 174. White to play. (1 move)
How can White live in a seki?

Section 4. Ko

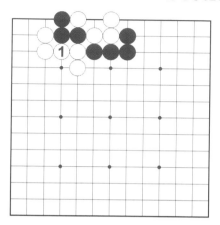

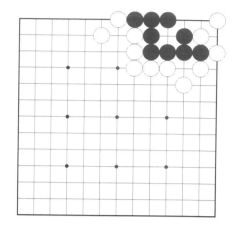

Problem 175. Black to play. (1 move)

After White 1, how can Black start a ko?

Problem 176. Black to play. (2 moves)

The only way Black can live is to start a ko.

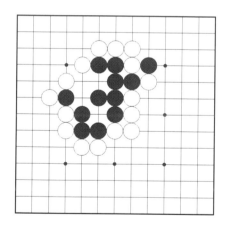

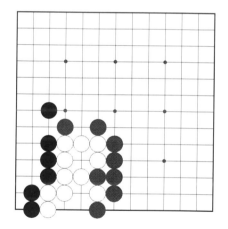

Problem 177. Black to play. (2 moves)

The only way Black can live is to start a ko.

Problem 178. White to play. (2 moves)

How can White start a ko?

Section 6. Capturing Races

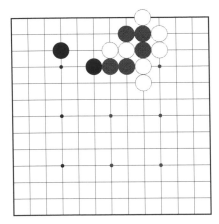

Problem 179. Black to play. (1 move)
How can Black capture two stones?

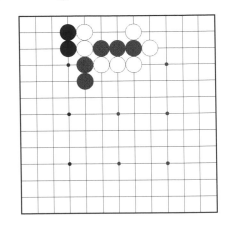

Problem 180. Black to play. (1 move)
How can Black capture two stones?

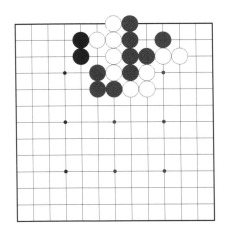

Problem 181. White to play. (3 moves)
How can White capture five stones?

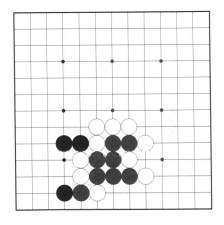

Problem 182. White to play. (3 moves)
How can White capture seven stones?

Introductory Problems
Level Four

Section 1. Atari

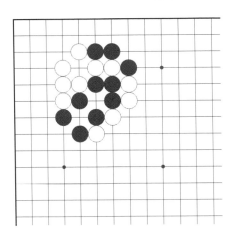

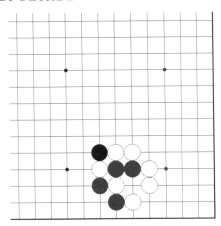

Problem 183. Black to play.

Three black stones are in atari. What should Black do?

Problem 184. Black to play.

Black has two ways to capture. Which way is best?

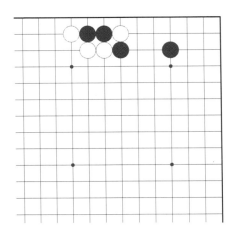

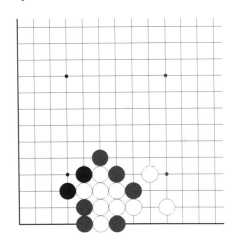

Problem 185. Black to play.

From which direction should Black atari?

Problem 186. Black to play.

From which direction should Black atari?

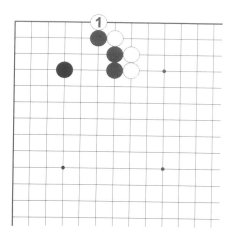

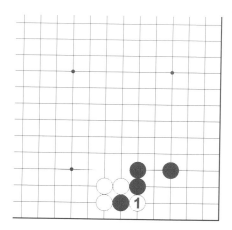

Problem 187. Black to play.

White 1 is a bad move. How should Black respond?

Problem 188. Black to play.

How should Black respond to White 1?

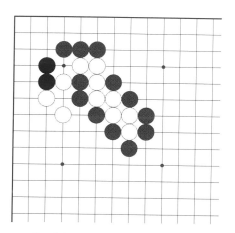

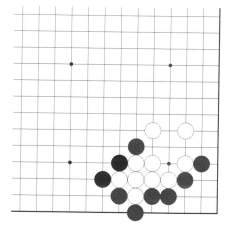

Problem 189. Black to play.

Eight white stones are caught in a ladder. On which point should Black atari?

Problem 190. Black to play.

How can Black capture seven stones?

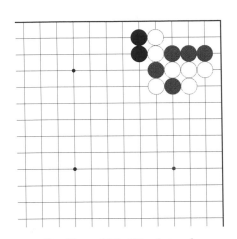

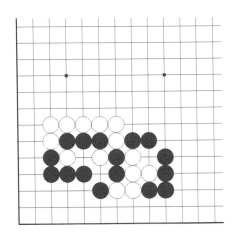

Problem 191. Black to play.

Two black stones are in atari. Which one should Black rescue?

Problem 192. Black to play.

A group of two and a group of three black stones are in atari. Which group should Black rescue?

Section 2. Capturing Races

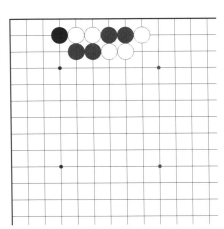

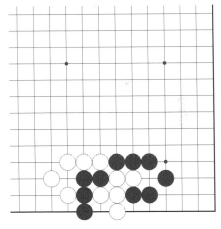

Problem 193. Black to play.

How can Black capture two stones?

Problem 194. Black to play.

How can Black capture five stones? (There are two correct answers.)

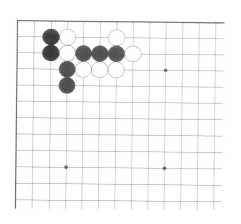

Problem 195. Black to play.
How can Black capture two stones?

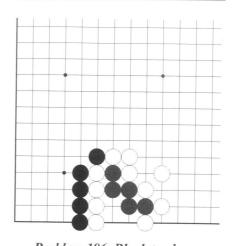

Problem 196. Black to play.
How can Black capture four stones?
(There are two correct answers.)

Section 3. Nets

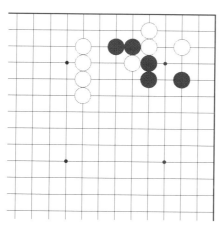

Problem 197. Black to play.
How can Black capture one stone?

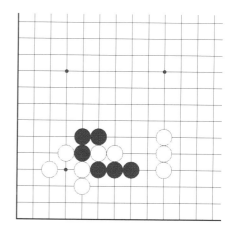

Problem 198. Black to play.
How can Black capture two stones?

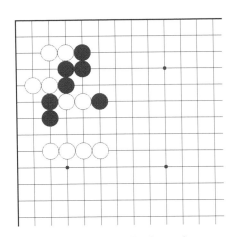

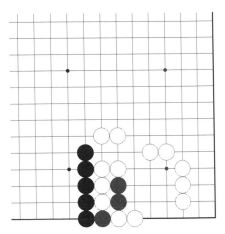

Problem 199. Black to play.
How can Black capture two stones?

Problem 200. Black to play.
How can Black capture two stones?

Section 4. Snapback

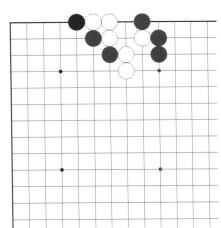

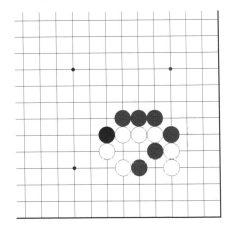

Problem 201. Black to play.
How can Black capture three stones?

Problem 202. Black to play.
How can Black capture three stones?

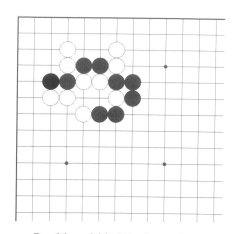

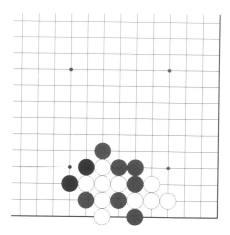

Problem 203. Black to play.
How can Black capture two stones?

Problem 204. Black to play.
How can Black capture six stones?

Section 5. Oiotoshi

(*Oiotoshi* — a move which ataries a group in such a way that no matter how it is defended, the group will still be in atari.)

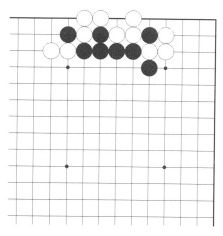

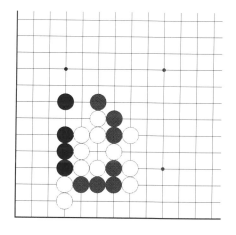

Problem 205. Black to play.
How can Black capture three stones?

Problem 206. Black to play.
How can Black capture six stones?

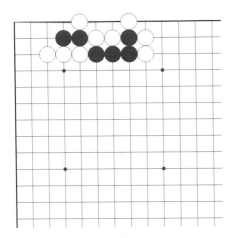

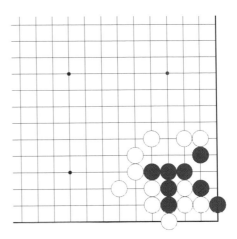

Problem 207. Black to play.
How can Black capture three stones?

Problem 208. Black to play.
How can Black capture three stones?

Section 6. Examples of Bad Moves

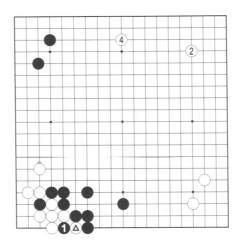

Problem 209. Which side has profited.
(Black 3 at the marked stone)

Black has captured and connected the ko with 1 and 3, while White has occupied an empty corner with 2 and extended along the top with 4. Which side has gained the most in this sequence?

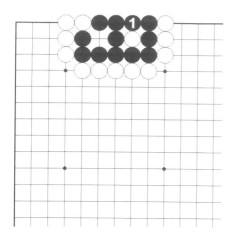

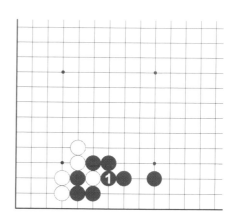

Problem 210. Good or bad?

Black has captured a stone with 1. Is this a good or a bad move?

Problem 211. Good or bad?

Black has captured a stone with 1. Is this a good or a bad move?

Section 7. Seki

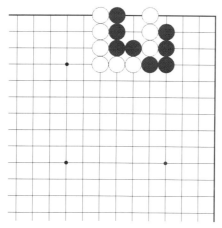

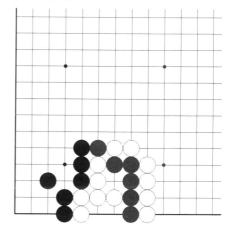

Problem 212. Black to play.

How can Black create a seki?

Problem 213. Black to play.

How can Black create a seki?

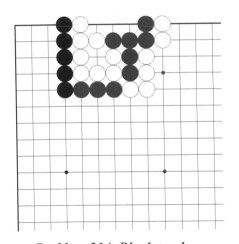

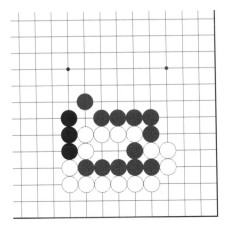

Problem 214. Black to play.
How can Black create a seki?

Problem 215. Black to play.
How can Black create a seki?

Section 8. Separating and Linking up Stones

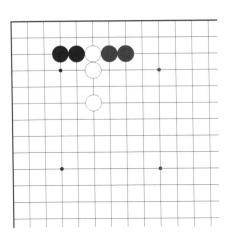

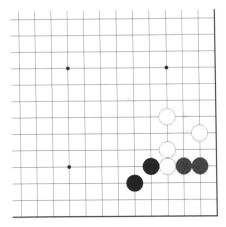

Problem 216. Black to play.
How can Black link up his two groups?

Problem 217. Black to play.
How can Black link up his two groups?

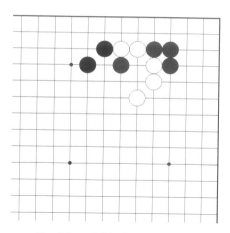

Problem 218. Black to play.
How can Black link up his stones?

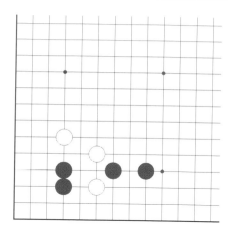

Problem 219. Black to play.
How can Black link up his stones?

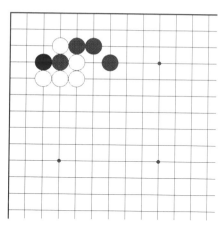

Problem 220. Black to play.
How can Black link up his stones?

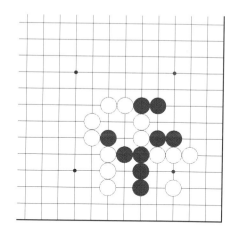

Problem 221. Black to play.
How can Black link up his stones?

Section 9. Life and Death

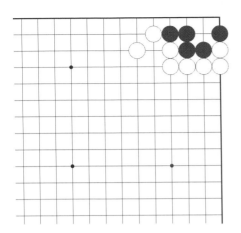

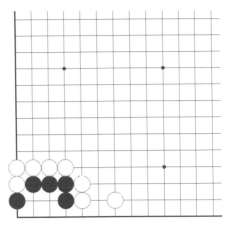

Problem 222. Black to play.

How can Black make two eyes and life?

Problem 223. Black to play.

How can Black make two eyes and life?

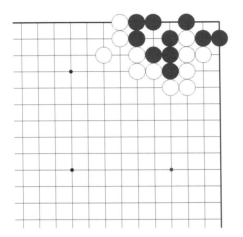

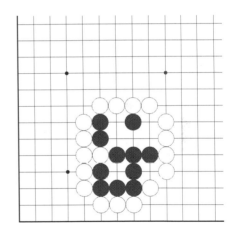

Problem 224. Black to play.

How can Black make two eyes and life?

Problem 225. Black to play.

How can Black make two eyes and life?

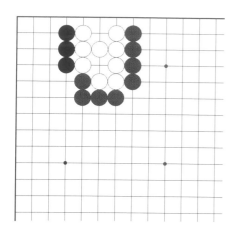

Problem 226. Black to play.

How can Black kill the white group?

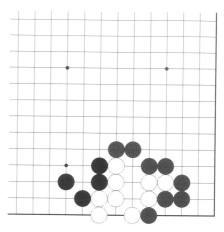

Problem 227. Black to play.

How can Black kill the white group?

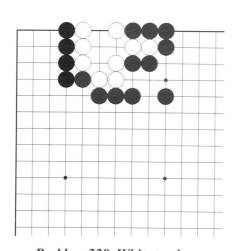

Problem 228. White to play.

How can White make two eyes and life?

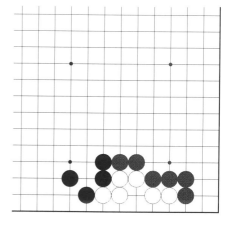

Problem 229. White to play.

How can White make two eyes and life?

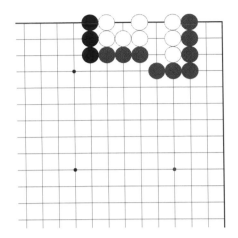

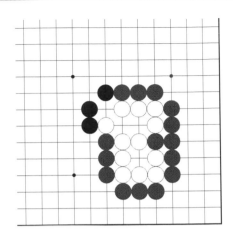

Problem 230. Black to play.
How can Black kill the white group?

Problem 231. Black to play.
How can Black kill the white group?

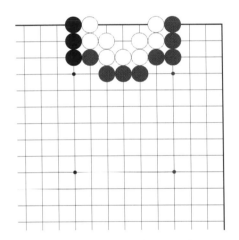

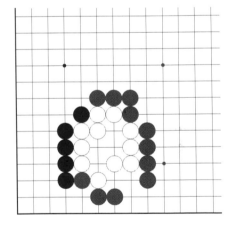

Problem 232. White to play.
How can White make two eyes and life?

Problem 233. White to play.
How can White make two eyes and life?

Section 10. How to Play in the Opening

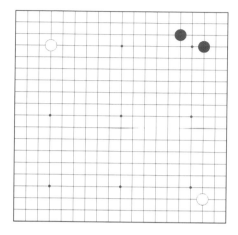

Problem 234. Black to Play

Where should Black play his next move? (There is more than one correct answer.)

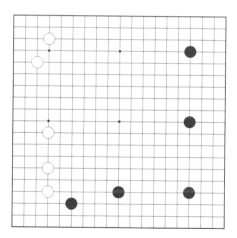

Problem 235. Black to Play

Where should Black play his next move? (There is more than one correct answer.)

Section 11. The Endgame

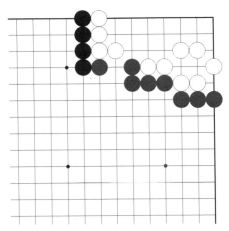

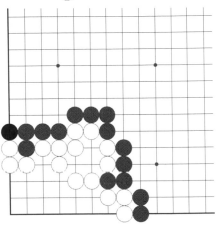

Problem 236. Black to play.

White needs a move to completely secure his territory. Where should he play?

Problem 237. Black to play.

White needs a move to completely secure his territory. Where should he play?

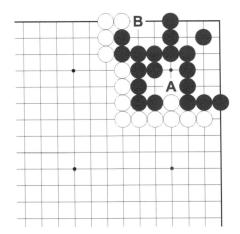

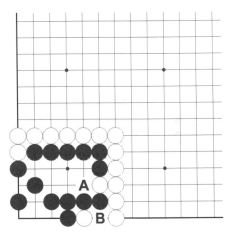

Problem 238. Which is bigger?

Which is the bigger move for either Black or White, A or B?

Problem 239. Which is bigger?

Which is the bigger move for either Black or White, A or B?

Part Two

Answers

Problem 1

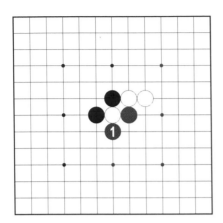
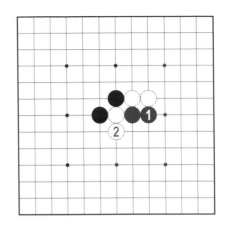

Correct Answer

Black can capture a stone by playing on White's last liberty with 1.

Wrong Answer

If Black plays any other move, such as 1, White can escape by extending 2.

Problem 2

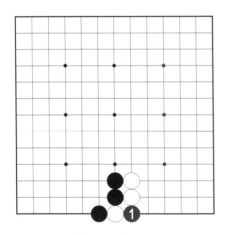
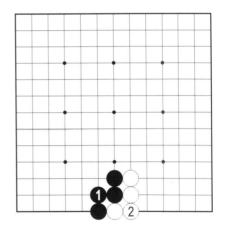

Correct Answer

Black can capture a stone by playing 1.

Wrong Answer

If Black connects with 1, White can save his stone by connecting with 2.

Problem 3

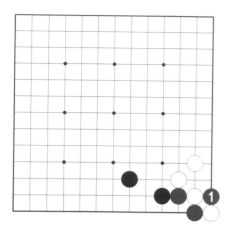

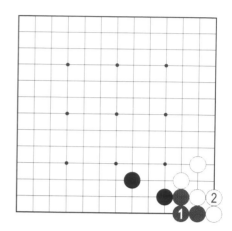

Correct Answer
Black can capture the white stone in the corner with 1.

Wrong Answer
If Black connects with 1, White can save his stone by connecting at 2.

Problem 4

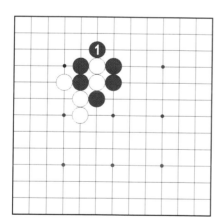

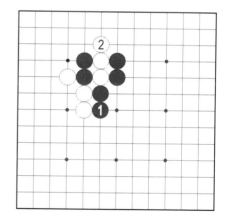

Correct Answer
Black can capture two stones by playing on their last liberty with 1.

Wrong Answer
If Black plays any other move, such as 1, White can save his stones by extending to 2.

Problem 5

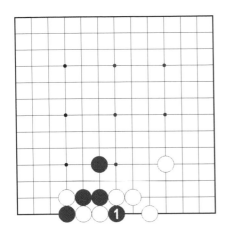

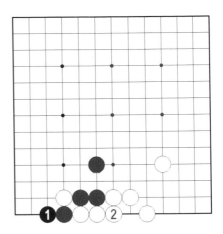

Correct Answer

By playing 1, Black can capture two stones.

Wrong Answer

If Black extends to 1, White saves his two stones by connecting at 2.

Problem 6

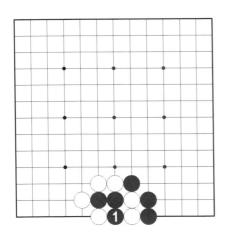

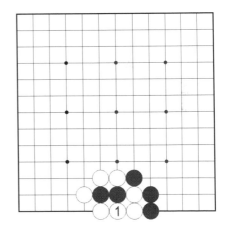

Correct Answer

By playing 1, Black can capture two stones.

If White plays first

If it's White's turn, he can capture two stones with 1.

Problem 7

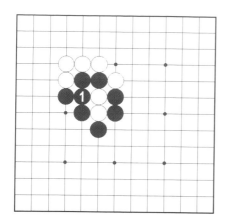 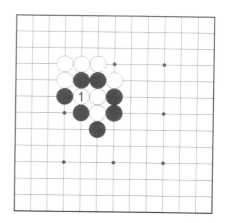

Correct Answer
By playing 1, Black can capture two stones.

If White plays first
If it's White's turn, it is White who captures two stones.

Problem 8

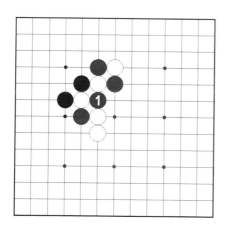 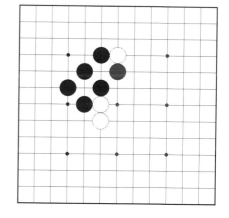

Correct Answer
By playing 1, Black simultaneously captures two stones.

The Resulting Shape
This is what the position looks like after the capture.

Problem 9

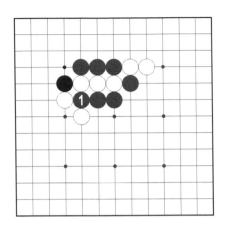

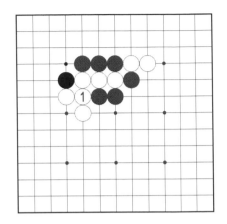

Correct Answer

By playing 1, Black can capture three stones.

If White plays first

If it's White's turn, he can rescue his three stones by connecting at 1.

Problem 10

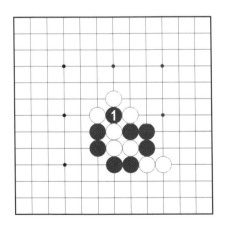

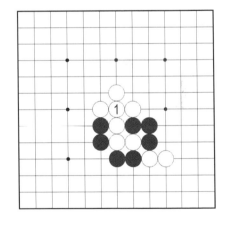

Correct Answer

Black 1 captures three stones.

If White plays first

If it's White's turn, he can rescue his three stones by connecting at 1.

Problem 11

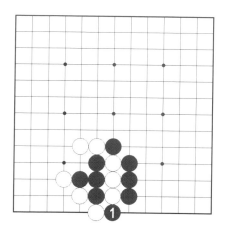

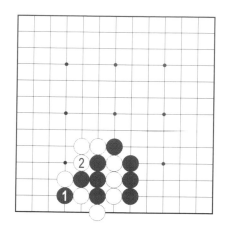

Correct Answer

By playing 1, Black can capture three stones.

Wrong Answer

If Black ataries with 1, White can capture four stones with 2.

Problem 12

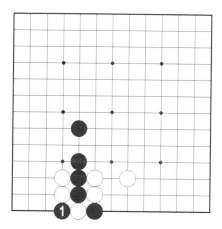

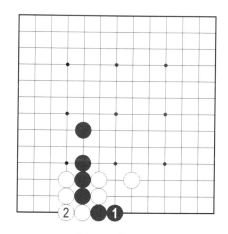

Correct Answer

Black can capture a stone by playing 1.

Wrong Answer

If Black extends to 1, White connects with 2 and his stones can't be captured.

Problem 13

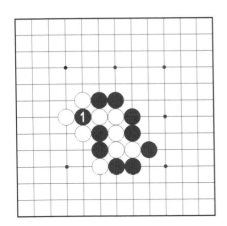

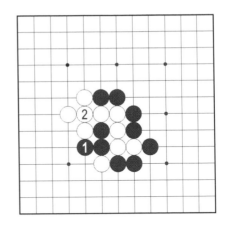

Correct Answer
Black can capture five stones by playing 1.

Wrong Answer
If Black plays 1, White connects at 2 and his stones can't be captured.

Problem 14

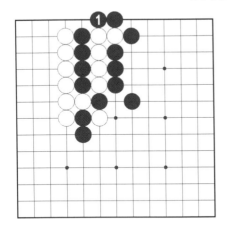

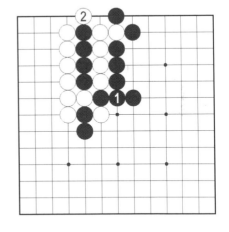

Correct Answer
Black can capture five stones by playing 1.

Wrong Answer
If Black connects with 1, it is White who captures four stones with 2.

Problem 15

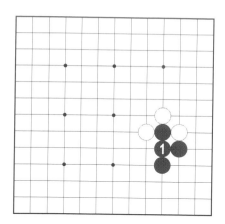

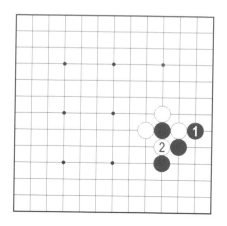

Correct Answer

Black can save his stone by connecting with 1.

Wrong Answer

If Black threatens to capture a stone with the atari of 1, White captures a stone with 2.

Problem 16

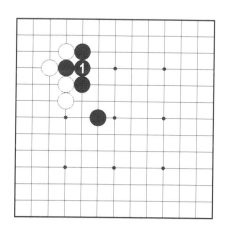

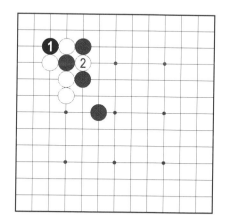

Correct Answer

Black can save his stone by connecting at 1.

Wrong Answer

If Black threatens to capture a stone by playing 1, White captures with 2.

Problem 17

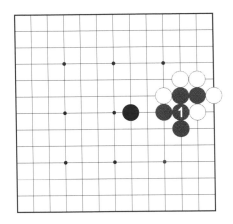

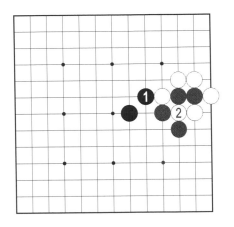

Correct Answer

Black can save his two stones by connecting at 1.

Wrong Answer

If Black ataries with 1, White will capture two stones with 2.

Problem 18

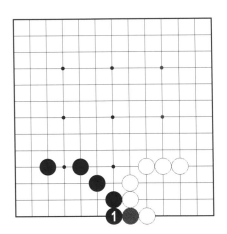

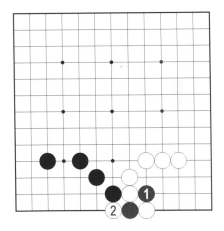

Correct Answer

Black can rescue his stone by connecting with 1.

Wrong Answer

Black 1 is unreasonable, since White will capture the black stone with 2.

Problem 19

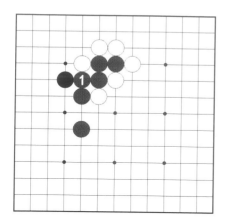 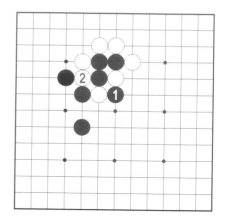

Correct Answer

Black can save his three stones by connecting at 1.

Wrong Answer

Black 1 is unreasonable, as White will capture the three stones with 2.

Problem 20

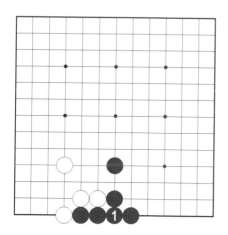 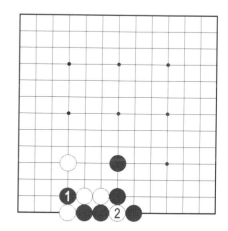

Correct Answer

Black can rescue his two stones by connecting at 1.

Wrong Answer

Black 1 is unreasonable, as White will capture two stones with 2.

Problem 21

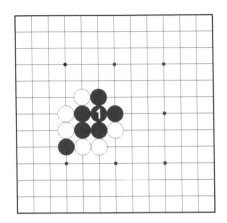

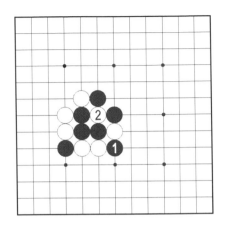

Correct Answer
Black can save his three stones by connecting at 1.

Wrong Answer
Black 1 is unreasonable, as White will capture three stones with 2.

Problem 22

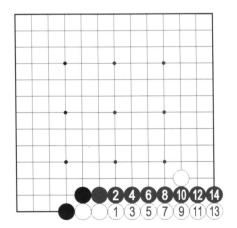

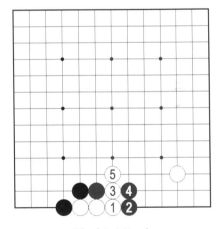

White can't rescue his stones.
White can't save his stones. If he persists with the moves to 13, his stones will be captured when Black plays 14.

Black's Mistake
After White 1, the atari of Black 2 is played in the wrong direction. White can escape with 3 and 5.

Problem 23

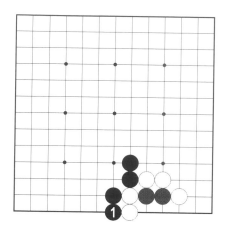

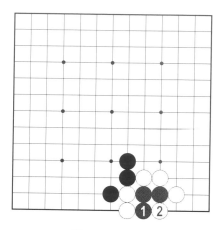

Correct Answer

If Black ataries with 1, the two white stone can't escape.

Wrong Answer

The atari of Black 1 is the wrong direction, White 2 captures three stones.

Problem 24

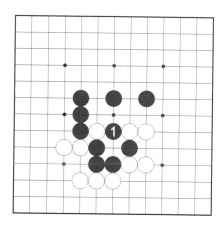

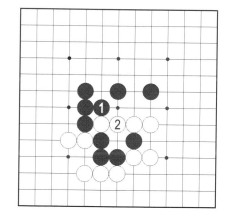

Correct Answer

If Black ataries with 1, the lone white stone can't escape.

Wrong Answer

If Black ataries with 1, White connects with 2 and Black's four stones below are dead.

Problem 25

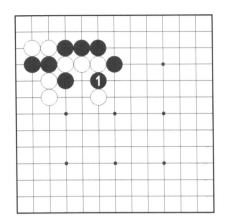

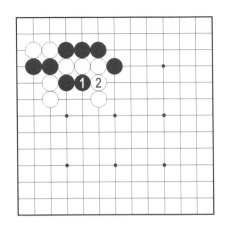

Correct Answer

Black can capture three stones with an atari at 1.

Wrong Answer

If Black ataries with 1, White connects at 2 and his stones can't be captured.

Problem 26

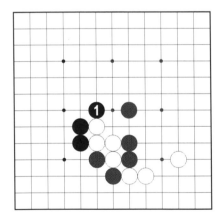

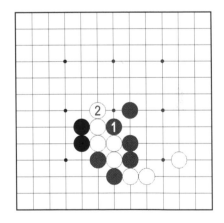

Correct Answer

Black can capture four stones with an atari at 1.

Wrong Answer

Black 1 is played in the wrong direction. White escapes by extending to 2.

Problem 27

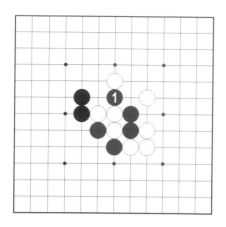

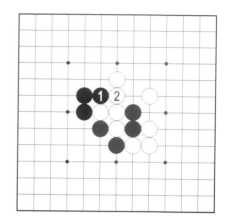

Correct Answer

Black can capture three stones with the atari of 1.

Wrong Answer

If Black ataries with 1, White connects at 2 and his stones have escaped.

Problem 28

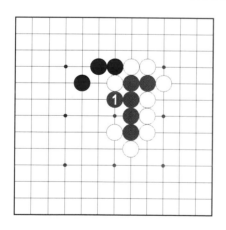

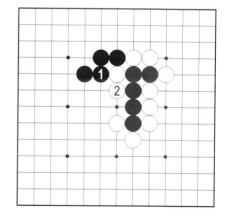

Correct Answer

If Black ataries with 1, the lone white stone can't escape.

Wrong Answer

The atari of Black 1 is played in the wrong direction. White will capture five stones after he ataries with 2.

Problem 29

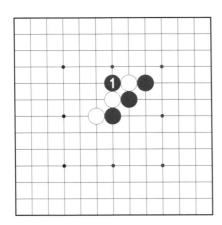

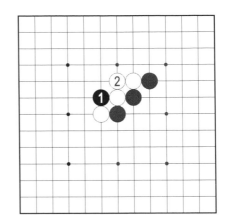

Correct Answer
Black 1 is a double atari. One of the two threatened white stones will be captured.

Wrong Answer
If Black ataries with 1, White connects with 2 and Black can't capture anything.

Problem 30

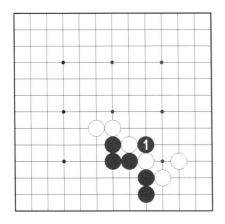

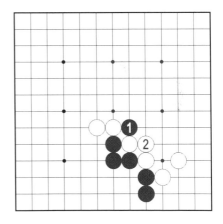

Correct Answer
Black 1 is a double atari. One of the two threatened white stones will be captured.

Wrong Answer
If Black ataries with 1, White connects with 2 and Black can't capture anything.

Problem 31

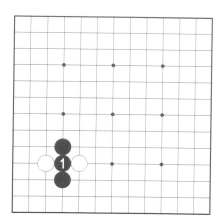

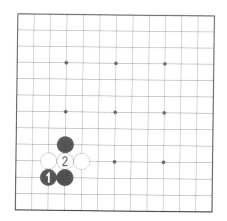

Correct Answer

Black can link up his stones with 1. White's two stones are now separated and Black has the advantage.

Wrong Answer

If Black plays 1, it is White who separates Black and links up his own stones with 2. White now has the advantage.

Problem 32

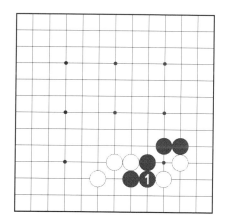

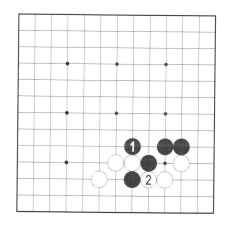

Correct Answer

By connecting at 1, Black links up his stones into one strong group.

Wrong Answer

Black 1 lets White cuts with 2, Black's stone on the third line can be captured, so White secures the territory at the bottom.

Problem 33

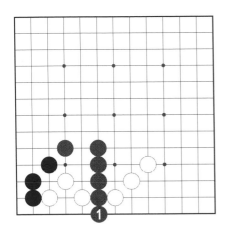

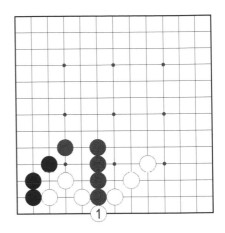

Correct Answer

When Black plays 1, White can't link up his stones. Playing to the left or right of 1 also prevents White from linking up.

If White plays first

If it were White's turn, he could link up his stones by playing underneath with 1.

Problem 34

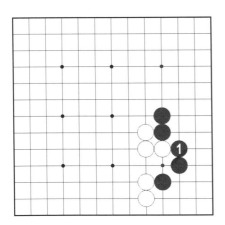

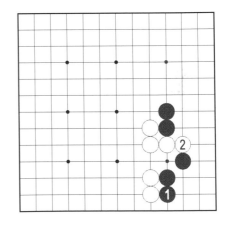

Correct Answer

By blocking with 1, Black links up his stones above and below to secure the territory on the right.

Wrong Answer

Black 1 lets White play 2. Black is no longer be able to link up and will end up with two weak groups.

Problem 35

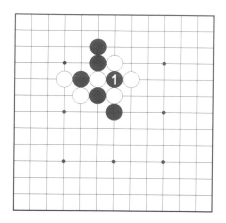

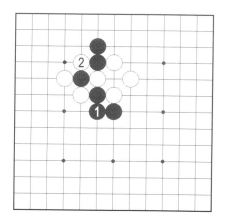

Correct Answer

Capturing the ko with Black 1 is the only way to fight back.

Wrong Answer

If Black connects with 1, White captures with 2 and Black's stones are separated.

Problem 36

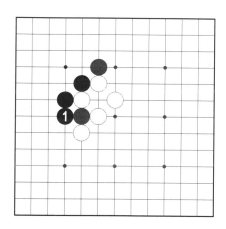

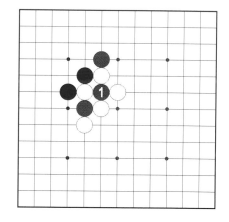

Correct Answer

In this case, Black should connect with 1, as he can't recapture the ko.

An illegal move

Black can't recapture with 1, as this is against the rules. Black must play elsewhere before recapturing.

Problem 37

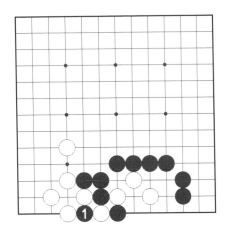

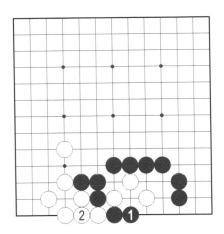

Correct Answer

Capturing the ko with Black 1 is the only move.

Wrong Answer

If Black extends to 1, White connects with 2 and the two black stones can't escape.

Problem 38

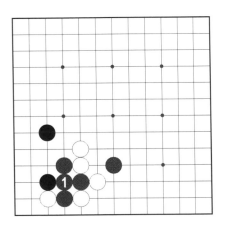

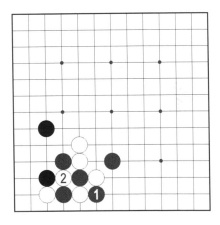

Correct Answer

Black should connect with 1, preventing White from starting a ko fight.

Wrong Answer

If Black ataries with 1, White starts a ko with 2. Black is now at a disadvantage.

Problem 39

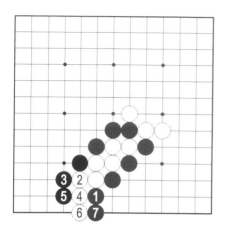

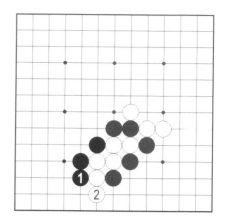

Correct Answer

If Black ataries with 1 to 5, White can't escape being captured in a ladder.

Wrong Answer

If Black ataries from the other side with 1, White can escape by extending to 2.

Problem 40

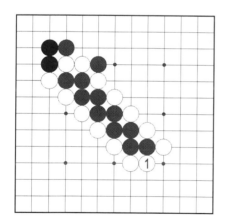

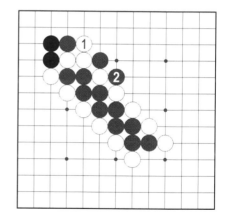

Correct Answer

If White captures ten stones with 1, Black no longer has a double atari on the white stones.

Wrong Answer

If White runs away with 1 to save his two stones in atari, Black captures and ataries with 2. The ten black stones are no longer in atari.

Problem 41

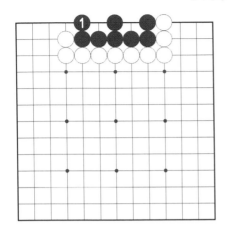
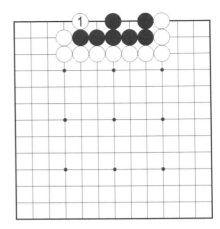

Correct Answer	*If White plays first*
Black can make two eyes and life for his group by playing 1.	If it is White's turn, the hane of White 1 will kill the black group.

Problem 42

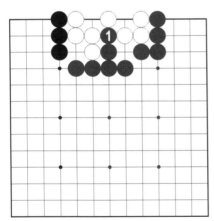
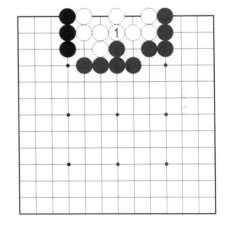

Correct Answer	*If White plays first*
Black 1 kills the white group. White now has two false eyes, so Black will be able to take these stones off the board at the end of the game.	If it's White's turn, he can make two eyes and life by connecting at 1.

Problem 43

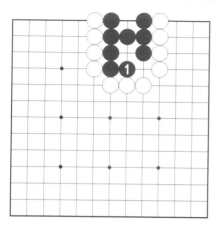 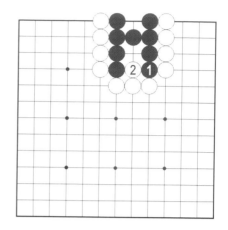

Correct Answer

Black can make two eyes and life for his group by playing 1.

Wrong Answer

Black 1 is a mistake. White plays 2 and Black can't make two eyes.

Problem 44

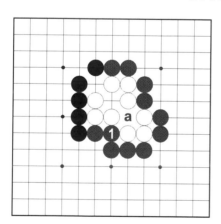 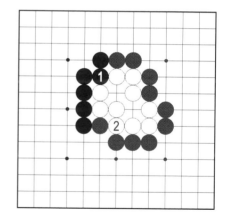

Correct Answer

Black 1 kills the white stones. White now has only one real eye and a false one at 'a', so Black will be able to take these stones off the board at the end of the game.

Wrong Answer

Black 1 is a mistake. White can make two eyes and life by connecting at 2.

Problem 45

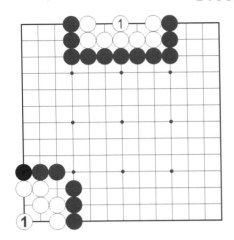

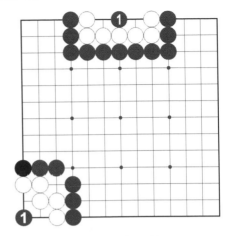

Correct Answer

Black can make two eyes in both positions by playing on the key point of 1.

If Black Plays First

Black 1 is the key point that kills both white groups.

Problem 46

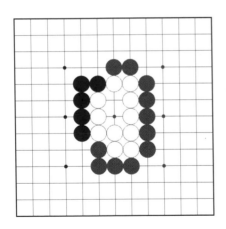

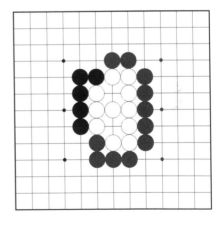

Correct Answer

White is dead. He has only one two-space eye, not two separated eyes.

Reference Diagram

In this position, White has two empty points, but, unlike the Correct Answer, they are separated, so White is alive.

Problem 47

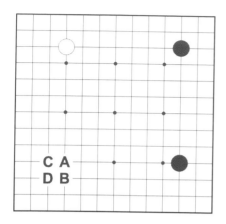

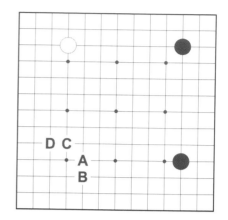

Correct Answer 1

Playing in an empty corner on any of the points A to D are good moves.

Correct Answer 2

Any one of the four moves, A to D, are also good.

Problem 48

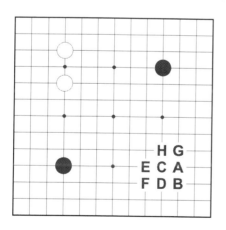

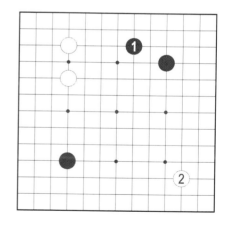

Correct Answer

Black should play in the empty corner on one of the points A to H. A move on any one of these points would be correct.

Wrong Answer

If Black 1, White occupies the empty corner with 2 and Black will be at a slight disadvantage. Occupying an empty corner usually takes priority over other moves.

Problem 49

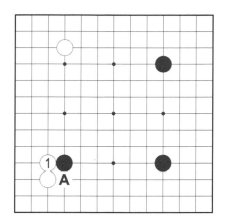

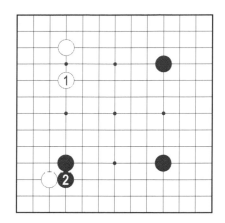

Correct Answer

Either White 1 or White A is the best move.

Wrong Answer

If White plays 1 or in another corner, Black 2 puts White at a disadvantage.

Problem 50

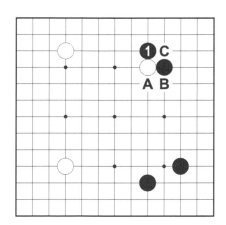

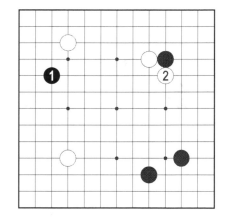

Correct Answer

Black 1 or any of the moves from A to C would be correct.

Wrong Answer

If Black plays 1 or on a point other than in the upper right corner, White 2 would put Black at a disadvantage.

Problem 51

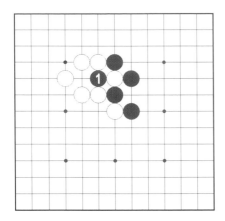 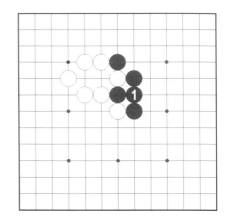

Correct Answer
Black should immediately capture a stone with 1.

Wrong Answer
Neglecting to capture and connecting with 1 is disadvantageous for Black.

Problem 52

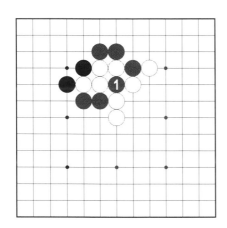 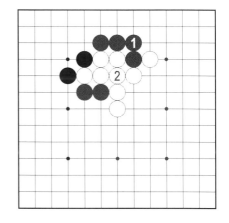

Correct Answer
Black should capture four stones with 1. This is an example of a snapback.

Wrong Answer
If Black connects with 1, White will save his four stones by playing 2.

Problem 53

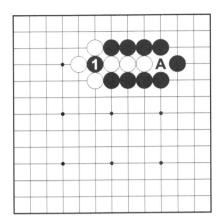

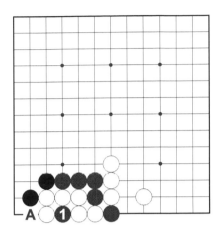

An illegal move

Black 1 is an illegal move. If the point A were occupied by either Black or White, then Black 1 would be possible.

An illegal move

Black 1 is also an illegal move. However, if Black occupies the point A, then Black could play 1 and capture six stones.

Problem 54

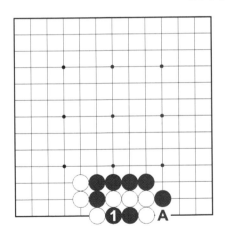

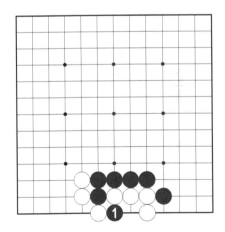

Correct Answer

Black 1 is an illegal move. However, if Black occupies the point A, Black 1 would capture four stones.

For Reference

In this position, Black 1 is a legal move.

Problem 55

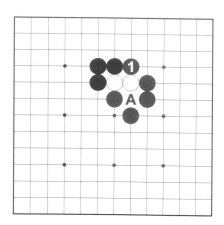

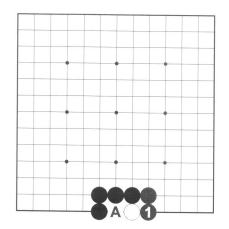

Black can't capture.

White's stones can't be removed from the board until the end of the game. If A were occupied by either Black or White, then Black 1 could capture.

Black can't capture.

The white stone can't be captured. As before, if A were occupied, Black 1 would capture the white stone.

Problem 56

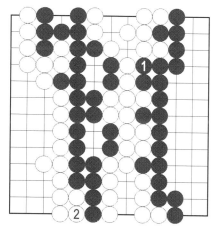

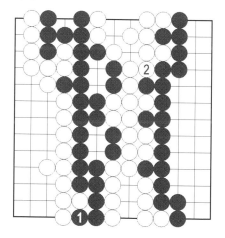

Correct Answer 1

There are two neutral points: Black 1 and White 2.

Correct Answer 2

The order of Black 1 and White 2 in this diagram has no effect on the score.

Problem 57

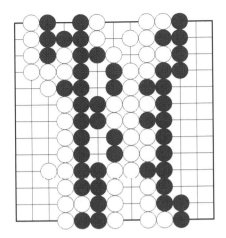

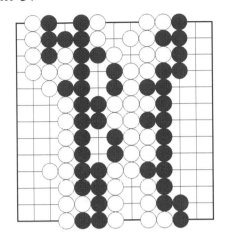

Black's territory

Black has 38 points of territory: 33 points on the right and 5 points in the middle.

Black wins by two points.

White has 36 points of territory: 29 points on the left and 7 points in the middle. Black wins by two points.

Problem 58

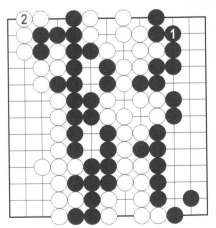

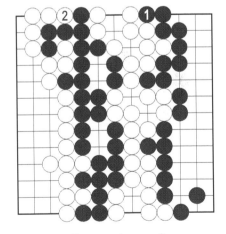

Correct Answer 1

Black 1 and White 2 are the last defensive moves of the game.

Correct Answer 2

The last two neutral points, Black 1 and White 2, can now be played.

Problem 59

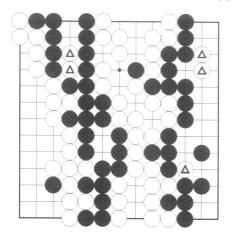

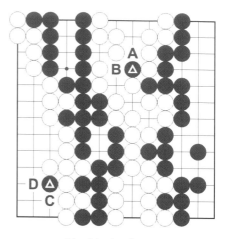

Correct Answer

The marked white stones are dead, so they can be removed from the board. And placed in White's territory.

Black's dead stones

The two marked black stones are also dead, so they may be removed from the board without playing the points A to D.

Problem 60

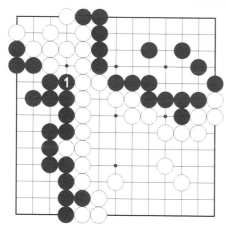

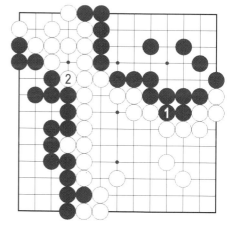

Correct Answer

Black 1 is the last remaining profitable point.

Wrong Answer

Black 1 is played on a neutral point, so White can take the last profitable point with 2. Black has lost a point.

Problem 61

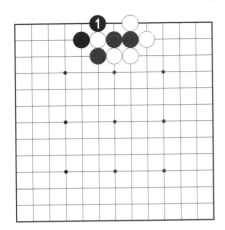

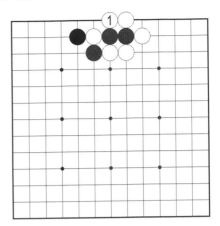

Correct Answer

By playing 1, Black captures a white stone.

If White Plays First

If it were White's turn, he would capture two stones with 1.

Problem 62

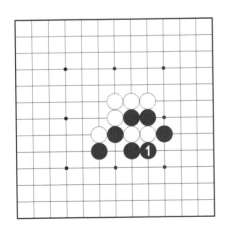

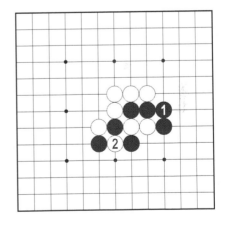

Correct Answer

By playing 1, Black can capture two stones.

Wrong Answer

If Black connects at 1, White captures with 2 and Black can no longer capture the two white stones.

Problem 63

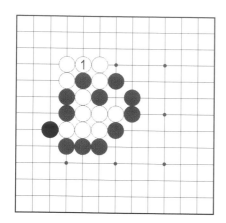

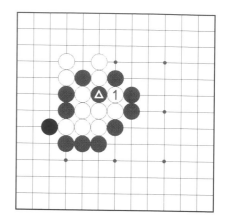

Correct Answer

Capturing a stone with White 1 is the only move.

Wrong Answer

Capturing with White 1 is wrong. Black can capture eight stones in a snapback by playing at the marked stone.

Problem 64

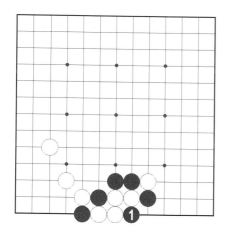

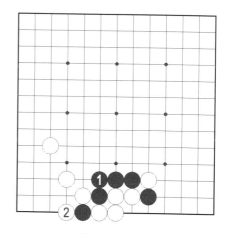

Correct Answer

By playing 1, Black can capture four stones.

Wrong Answer

If Black connects with 1, White captures with 2 and the four white stones can no longer be captured.

Problem 65

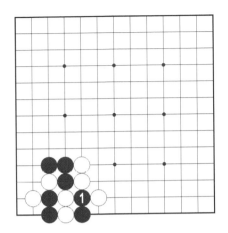

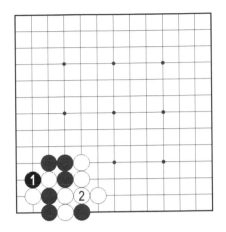

Correct Answer

If Black captures two stones with 1, the remaining two white stones in the corner can't escape.

Wrong Answer

If Black captures a stone with 1, White connects with 2 and rescues two of his stones.

Problem 66

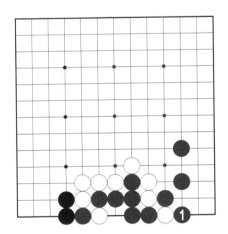

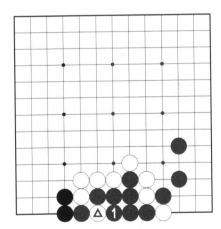

Correct Answer

Capturing the stone on the right with Black 1 is correct.

Wrong Answer

If Black captures the marked stone, he will lose seven stones in a snapback when White recaptures at the marked stone.

Problem 67

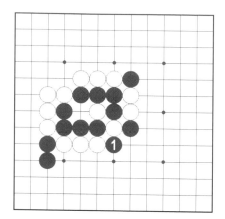

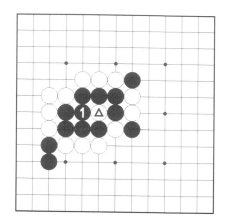

Correct Answer

Capturing a stone with Black 1 is the only move.

Wrong Answer

If Black captures a stone with 1, he will lose nine stones when White recaptures in a snapback at the marked stone.

Problem 68

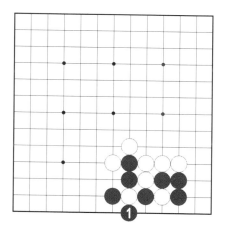

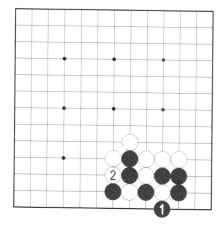

Correct Answer

Capturing the stone on the left with Black 1 is correct.

Wrong Answer

If Black captures the stone on the right, he will lose two stones when White plays 2.

Problem 69

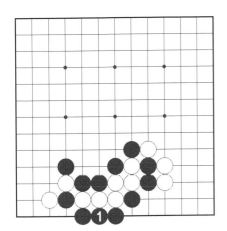

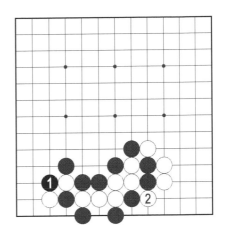

Correct Answer

Capturing six white stones with Black 1 is correct.

Wrong Answer

If Black captures a stone with 1, White captures two stones with 2 and the six white stones can no longer be captured.

Problem 70

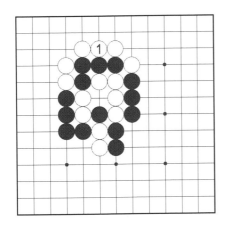

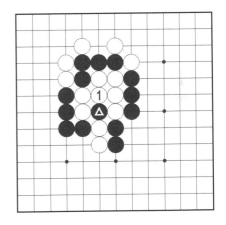

Correct Answer

Capturing four stones with White 1 is correct.

Wrong Answer

If White captures a stone with 1, Black will capture seven white stones in a snapback by playing at the marked stone.

Problem 71

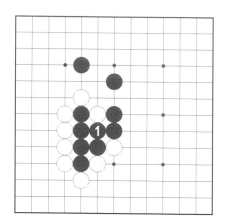

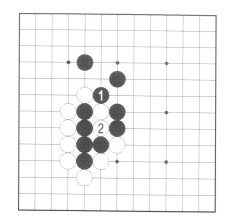

Correct Answer
Black should connect with 1, rescuing his five stones that are in atari.

Wrong Answer
If Black plays any other move, such as the atari of Black 1, White will capture five stones with 2.

Problem 72

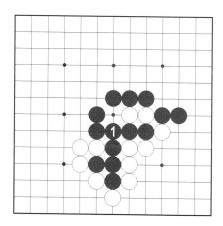

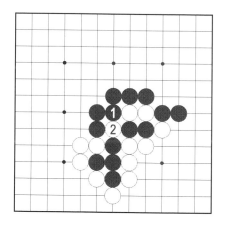

Correct Answer
Black should play 1, connecting his four stones in atari to the ones above.

Wrong Answer
If Black captures two stones with 1, White captures four stones with 2.

Problem 73

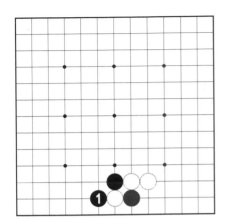

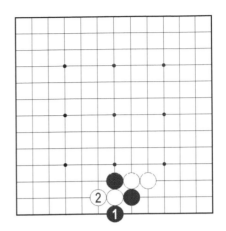

Correct Answer

If Black ataries with 1, the white stone will eventually be captured.

Wrong Answer

The atari of Black 1 from below is wrong. White extends to 2 and the black stones are the ones that will be captured.

Problem 74

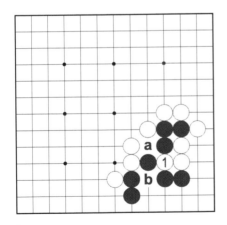

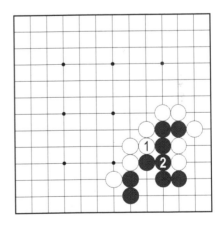

Correct Answer

If White ataries with 1, there is no way for Black to save his three stones. If Black connects at 'a', White captures at 'b'.

Wrong Answer

If White ataries from the other side with 1, Black's stones can't be captured after he connects with 2.

Problem 75

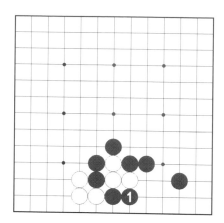

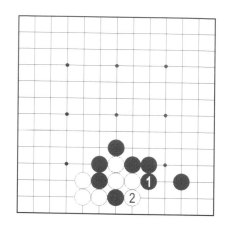

Correct Answer
If Black ataries with 1, there is no way that the three white stones can escape.

Wrong Answer
The atari of Black 1 is played in the wrong direction. White ataries with 2 and White's stones are safe.

Problem 76

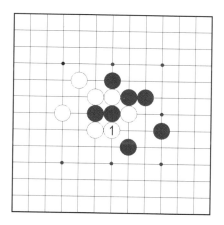

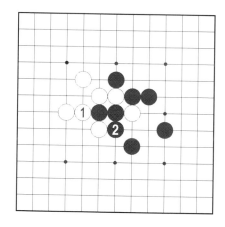

Correct Answer
The atari of White 1 is correct. The two black stones can't escape capture.

Wrong Answer
The atari of White 1 is in the wrong direction. After 2, Black's stones have escaped.

Problem 77

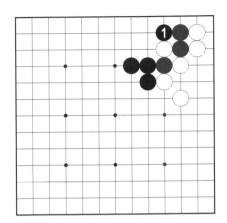 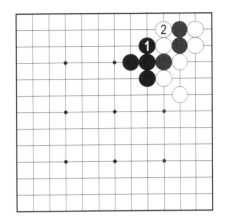

Correct Answer
Black should atari with 1. The lone white stone can't escape.

Wrong Answer
The atari of Black 1 is a mistake. White ataries with 2 and the two black stones in the corner will be captured.

Problem 78

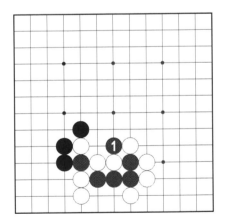 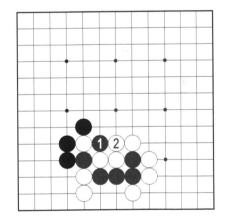

Correct Answer
Black 1 is the only move that can capture three stones.

Wrong Answer
The atari of Black 1 allows White to save two of his stones by connecting at 2.

Problem 79

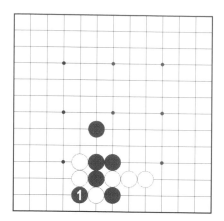

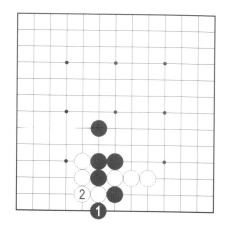

Correct Answer

After Black ataries with 1, the lone white stone at the bottom can't avoid being captured.

Wrong Answer

Black 1 forces White to connect with 2, letting him save his stone.

Problem 80

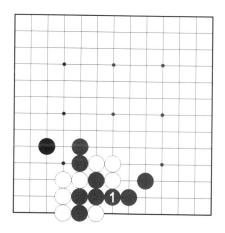

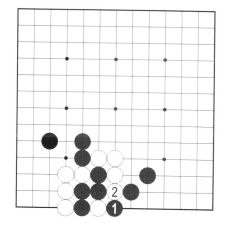

Correct Answer

Black should link up to his other stones by connecting with 1. The lone white stone on the first line is now trapped.

Wrong Answer

If Black captures with 1, White pushes in with 2 and the four black stones at the bottom will be captured.

Problem 81

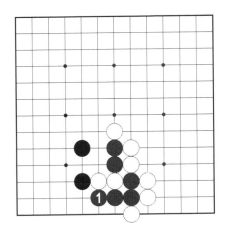

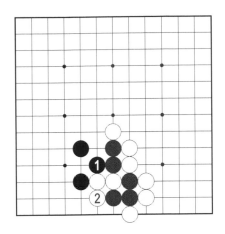

Correct Answer

If Black ataries from below with 1, the two white stones can't escape.

Wrong Answer

The atari of Black 1 from above lets White escape with 2 and capture three black stones.

Problem 82

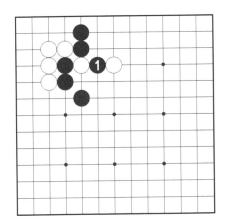

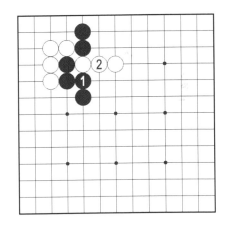

Correct Answer

Black 1 captures a stone and links up his own stones above and below.

Wrong Answer

If Black ataries with 1, White plays 2 and his stone can't be captured. However, Black's stones at the top are trapped.

Problem 83

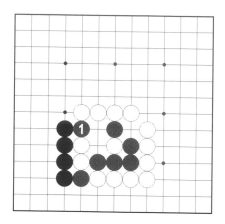 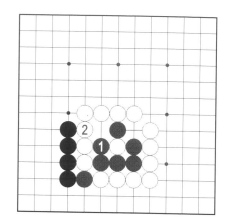

Correct Answer
Black should atari with 1. This move guarantees the capture of three stones.

Wrong Answer
If Black ataries with 1, White connects with 2. There is now no way that the black group in the center can live.

Problem 84

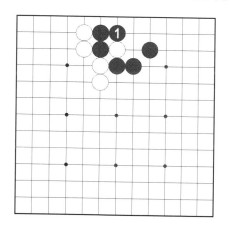 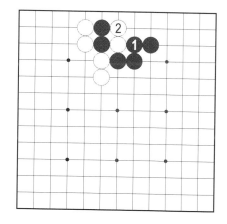

Correct Answer
Black 1 captures the white stone.

Wrong Answer
If Black ataries with 1, White escapes with 2 and captures two stones.

Problem 85

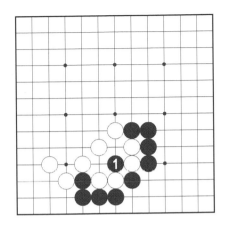

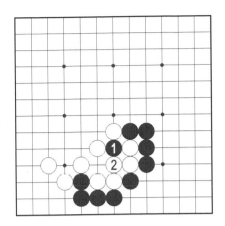

Correct Answer

Black 1 is a double atari. No matter how White responds, two of his stones will be captured.

Wrong Answer

Black 1 is a bad move. White 2 captures this stone and Black is left without a good move.

Problem 86

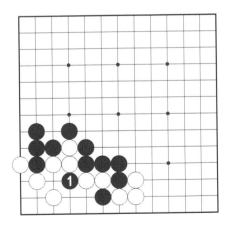

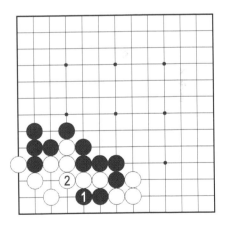

Correct Answer

Black 1 is a double atari. Black will capture either White's two-stone or three-stone group.

Wrong Answer

If Black ataries with 1, White secures all his stones by connecting at 2, leaving Black with no good follow-up moves.

Problem 87

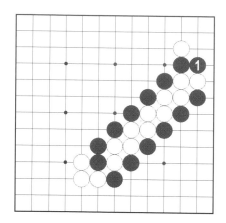

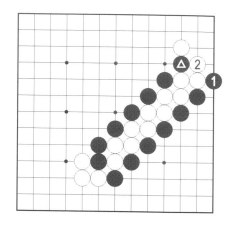

Correct Answer

Black 1 is the move that captures eleven white stones.

Wrong Answer

Black 1 here allows White to escape with 2. The marked stone is now in atari.

Problem 88

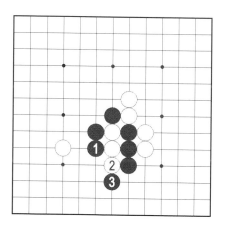

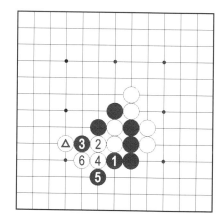

Correct Answer

Black 1 and 3 set up a ladder. The three white stones can't escape.

Wrong Answer

If Black immediately tries to capture with 1, the marked stone will break the ladder when White ataries with 6.

Problem 89

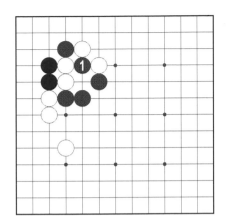

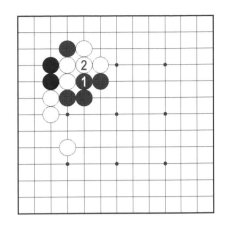

Correct Answer

Black 1 captures two stones in a snapback. There is now no way that White can save his two stones.

Wrong Answer

If Black ataries with 1, White saves his two stones by connecting at 2.

Problem 90

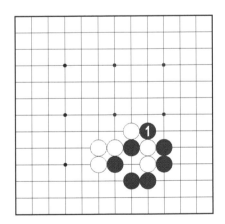

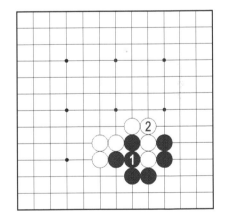

Correct Answer

The atari of Black 1 guarantees the capture of two white stones in a snapback.

Wrong Answer

The atari of Black 1 lets White save his two stones by connecting with 2.

Problem 91

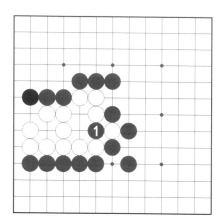

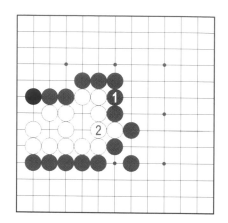

Correct Answer

Black should recapture with 1. White's stones can't make two eyes, so they are dead.

Wrong Answer

If Black connects 1, White connects with 2 and his group is alive with two eyes.

Problem 92

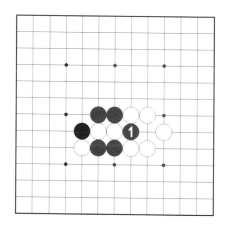

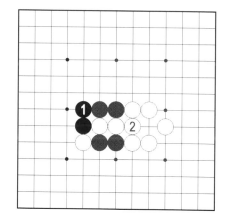

Correct Answer

Black should recapture two stones with 1.

Wrong Answer

If Black connects at 1, White can rescue his two stones by connecting with 2.

Problem 93

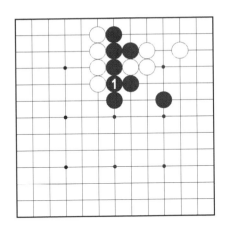

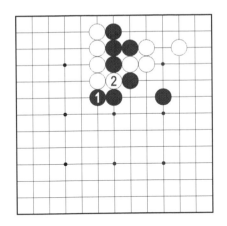

Correct Answer

Black can link up all his stones by connecting with 1.

Wrong Answer

If Black plays any other move, such as 1, White will cut with 2 and the four black stones at the top are dead.

Problem 94

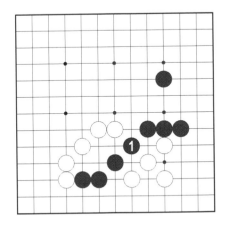

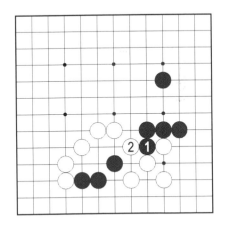

Correct Answer

Black can link up all of his stones by playing 1.

Wrong Answer

Black 1 does not work. When White plays 2, the three black stones at the bottom are cut off and dead.

Problem 95

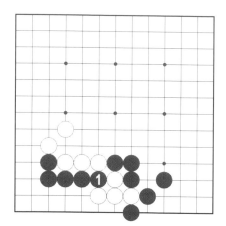

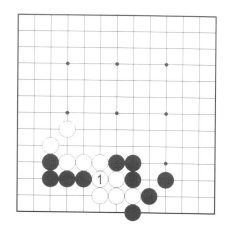

Correct Answer

Black 1 cuts off the four white stones from the ones above. They are now dead.

If White Plays First

If it is White's turn, he can link up his stones by connecting at 1.

Problem 96

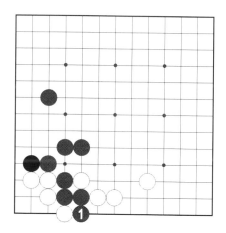

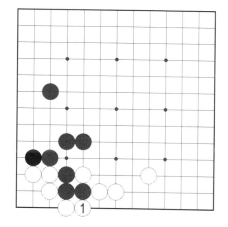

Correct Answer

Black 1 separates White into a four-stone group on the left and a four-stone group on the right. White is now unable to link up.

If White Plays First

If it is White's turn, he can link up all of his stones by playing 1.

Problem 97

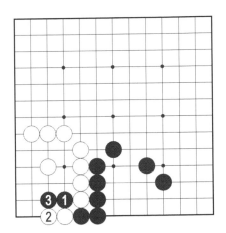

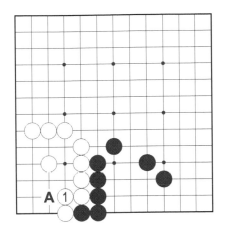

Correct Answer

If Black ataries with 1, White's stone on the first line can't escape. If White 2, Black 3 drives him into the corner.

If White Plays First

If it were White's turn, he would play at either 1 or A.

Problem 98

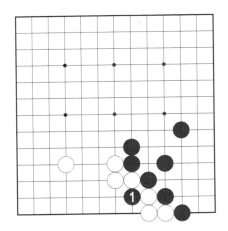

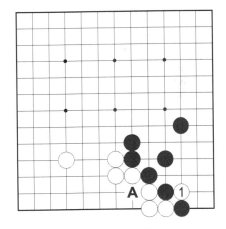

Correct Answer

Black should go after the three white stones with the atari of 1.

If White Plays First

If it were White's turn, he would play a double atari with 1. Black A is no longer effective.

Problem 99

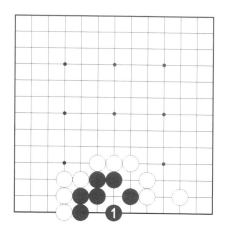

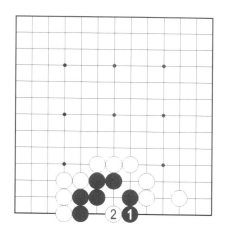

Correct Answer

Black 1 is the key point. Black now has two eyes, so his stones are alive.

Wrong Answer

If Black plays any other move, White will occupy the key point of 2, leaving Black with only one eye.

Problem 100

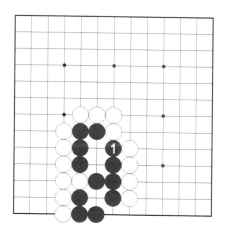

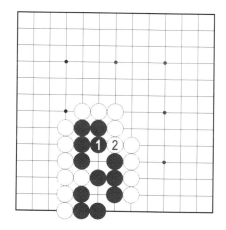

Correct Answer

If Black plays 1, he makes two eyes, so his stones are alive.

Wrong Answer

If Black plays 1, White 2 puts five stones into atari. The black group is dead.

Problem 101

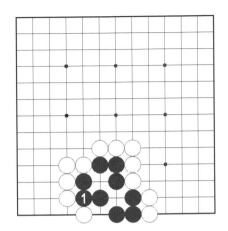

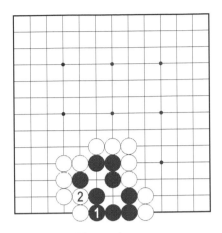

Correct Answer

Black 1 is the key point. Black now has two eyes, so his stones are alive.

Wrong Answer

Black 1 is a mistake. White plays on the key point of 2 and kills the black group.

Problem 102

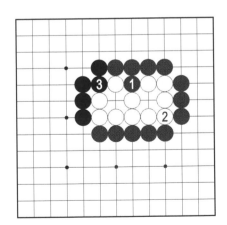

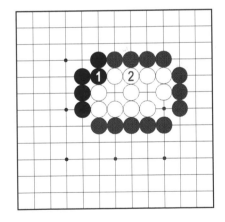

Correct Answer

Black 1 is the key point. If White make an eye with 2, Black 3 destroys White's eye on the left, so White's group is dead.

Wrong Answer

If Black first plays 1, White's stones are unconditionally alive after White takes the key point of 2.

Problem 103

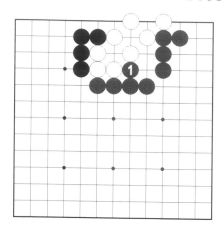 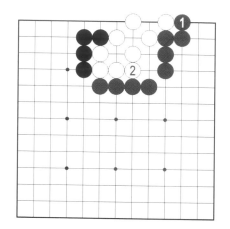

Correct Answer
Black 1 makes a false eye, so it is the key point for killing the white group.

Wrong Answer
If Black plays 1, White will play on the key point of 2 and his stones are alive.

Problem 104

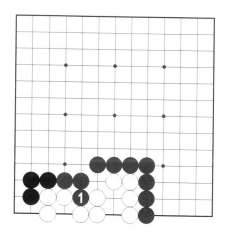 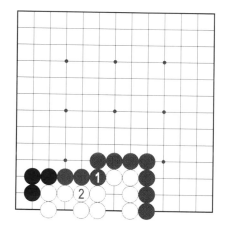

Correct Answer
Black 1 makes a false eye, so it is the key point for killing the white group.

Wrong Answer
If Black plays 1, White will play on the key point of 2 and his stones are alive.

Problem 105

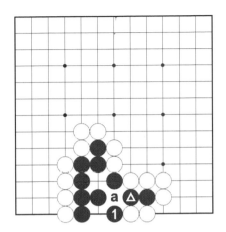

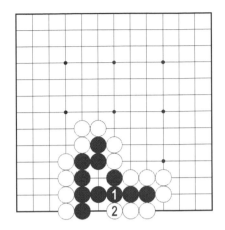

Correct Answer

Black 1 is the key move. If White captures two stones at 'a', Black will recapture at the marked stone and he is alive.

Wrong Answer

If Black connects at 1, defending his two endangered stones, White will play 2 and the black group is dead.

Problem 106

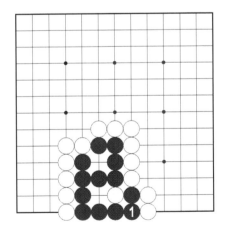

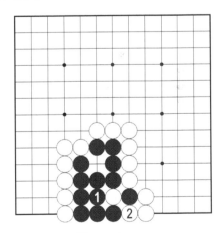

Correct Answer

If Black plays 1, his group has two eyes and is alive.

Wrong Answer

If Black captures a stone with 1, White makes a false eye with 2 and the black group is dead.

Problem 107

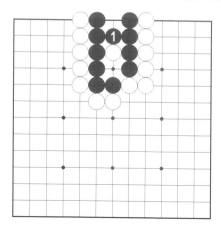 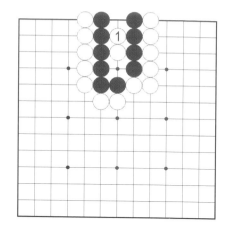

Correct Answer

If Black plays 1, he makes two eyes, so his group is alive.

If White Plays First

If it were White's turn, he would extend to 1 and kill the black group.

Problem 108

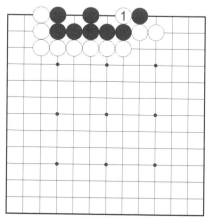 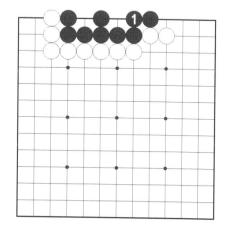

Correct Answer

White 1 makes a false eye, so the black group is dead.

If White Plays First

If it were Black's turn, connecting at 1 would give the black group two eyes and life.

Problem 109

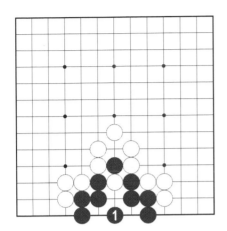

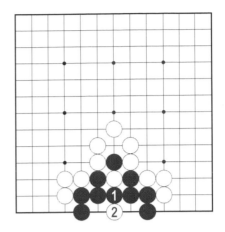

Correct Answer

Dipping down to Black 1 is the move that gives the black group two eyes.

Wrong Answer

If Black were to capture a stone with 1, White 2 would kill the black group by striking at the key point of 2.

Problem 110

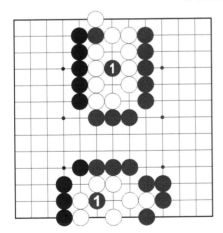

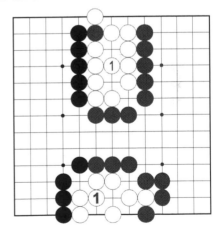

Correct Answer

Black 1 kills the white groups above and below.

If White Plays First

If it were White's turn, White 1 would make both his groups unconditionally alive with two eyes.

Problem 111

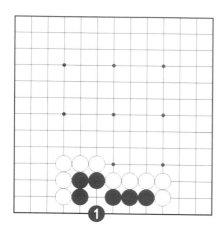

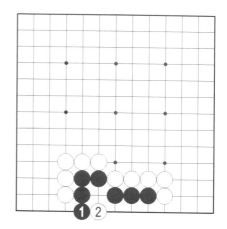

Correct Answer

Black 1 is the key move that gives the black group two eyes and life.

Wrong Answer

Black 1 lets White occupy the key point of 2. Black can't get two eyes, so his group dies.

Problem 112

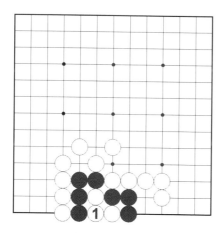

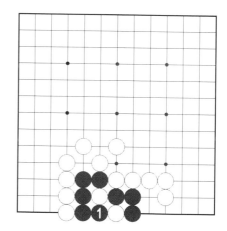

Correct Answer

Black would like to connect at 1 and leave Black with a dead three-space eye, but this is an illegal move. Therefore —

Reference

Black can capture two white stones with 1 whenever White fills a black liberty, so his group is unconditionally alive.

Problem 113

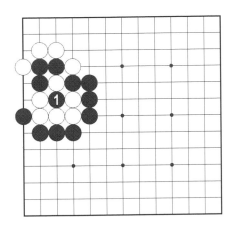 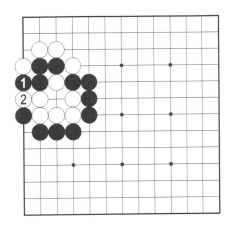

Correct Answer

The only way the Black can save his three stones is to start a ko with 1.

Wrong Answer

Trying to escape with Black 1 is futile. White will capture four stones with 2.

Problem 114

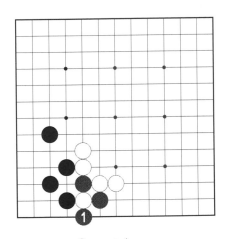 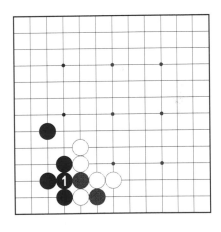

Correct Answer

Black should capture a stone with 1. This move resolves the ko.

Reference

Black 1 also resolves the ko, but even though Black will eventually take the white stone, the result is less than satisfactory, as Black has wasted a move.

Problem 115

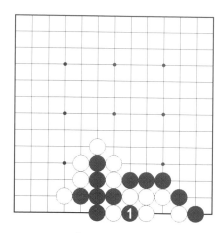

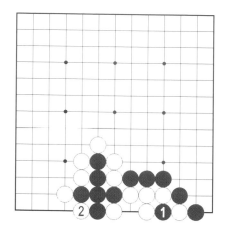

Correct Answer

Capturing a stone in a ko with 1 is the only way that Black can rescue his six stones in atari.

Wrong Answer

Capturing on the right with Black 1 is also a ko, but the focus of the fight is on the left, so White 2 captures six stones.

Problem 116

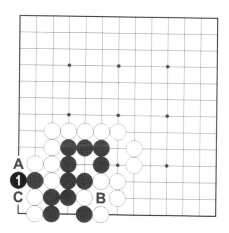

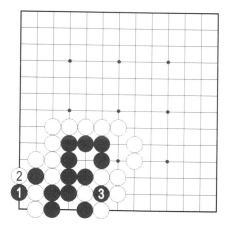

Correct Answer

Black 1 is a ko threat. If White A next, Black captures the ko with B. If the ko continues, Black has two more ko threats at C.

Reference

Black 1 is also a ko threat, but there is no follow-up ko threat after White 2. In any case, Black can continue the ko with 3.

Problem 117

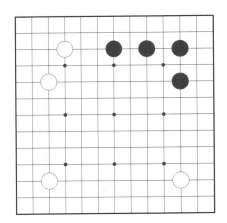

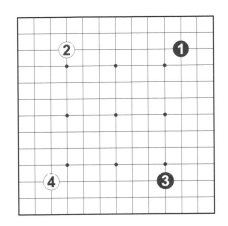

Correct Answer

Since White has occupied three of the four corners, his position is superior to Black's.

A Normal Opening

This is a normal way to play the opening. Each side occupies two corners.

Problem 118

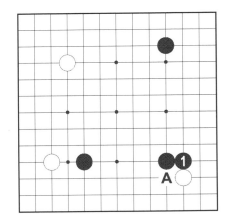

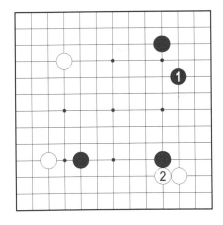

Correct Answer

Either Black 1 or Black A is the correct answer.

Wrong Answer

If Black plays 1, White will extend to 2 and Black will be at a disadvantage.

Problem 119

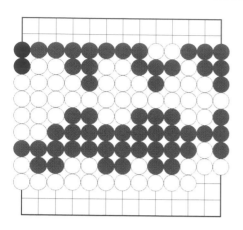 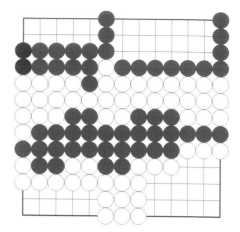

Correct Answer 1

You should arrange the territories so the stones are disturbed as little as possible. White and Black have 28 points each.

Correct Answer 2

This arrangement of territories is also correct and gives the same result. Black and White have 28 points, so the result is a draw.

Problem 120

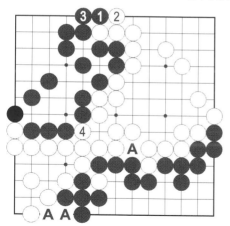 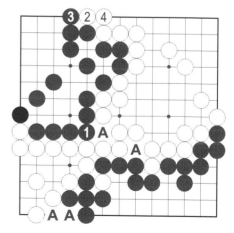

Correct Answer

Black 1 to 3 and White 4 are the last profitable points. The points marked A are neutral points and have no value.

Reference Diagram

As the problem was stated, Black 1 to 4 are also correct, but White is better by one point. The points A are neutral points.

Problem 121

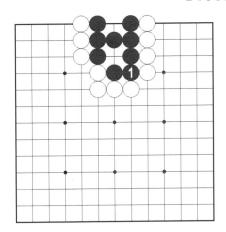 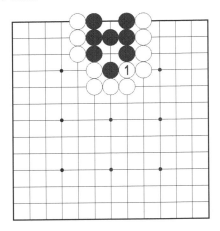

Correct Answer

By playing 1, Black makes two eyes. Black has no other way to live.

If White Plays First

If it were White's turn, he would play 1 and Black's lower eye would become a false one.

Problem 122

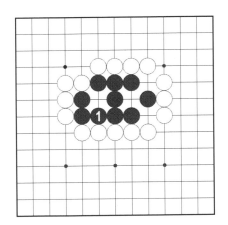 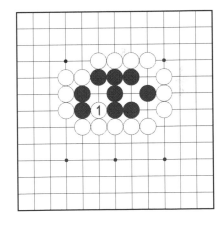

Correct Answer

By playing 1, Black makes two eyes and lives. There is no other move if Black wants to live.

If White Plays First

If it were White's turn, he would play 1 and Black's group would have only one eye.

Problem 123

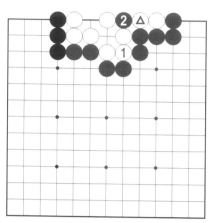
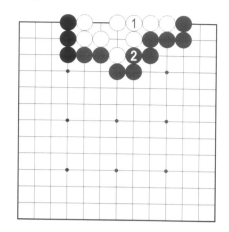

Correct Answer

White 1 should make an eye with 1. If Black captures two stones with 2, White retakes with 3 (at the marked stone).

Wrong Answer

If White connects with 1, Black 2 turns White's eye on the second line into a false one, so White is dead.

Problem 124

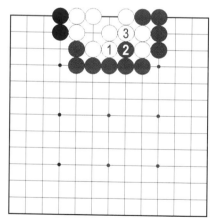
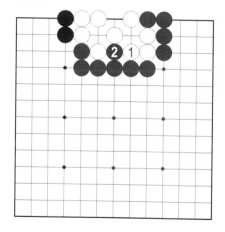

Correct Answer

White 1 makes an eye on the left. If Black 2, White 3 defends his eye on the right.

Wrong Answer

If White plays 1, Black 2 turns White's eyes on the left and the right into false ones. White is left with only one real eye.

Problem 125

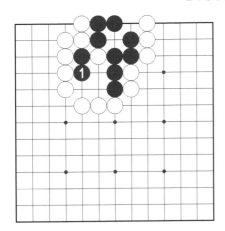 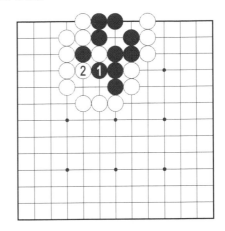

Correct Answer

Black 1 makes an eye where the isolated white stone is. Black now has two eyes, so he lives.

Wrong Answer

Capturing a stone with Black 1 lets White atari with 2. Black now has only one eye, so his group dies.

Problem 126

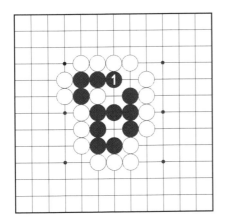 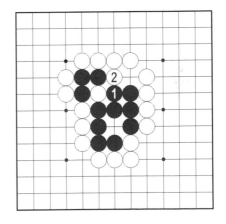

Correct Answer

Black 1 makes an eye where the isolated white stone is. This move gives Black two eyes, so he lives.

Wrong Answer

If Black captures with 1, White 2 puts three stones into atari, so the black group dies.

Problem 127

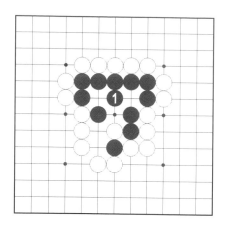

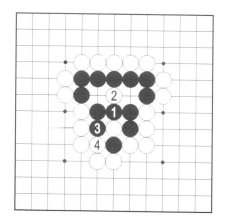

Correct Answer

Black 1 makes two eyes, one on the left and one on the right.

Wrong Answer

Black 1 lets White play on the key point of 2. After the exchange of 3 for White 4, Black can't make two eyes.

Problem 128

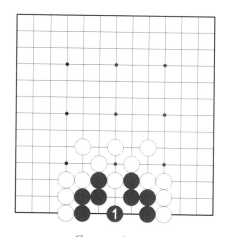

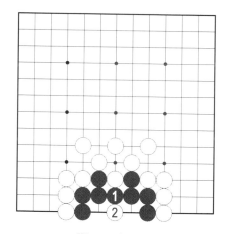

Correct Answer

If Black dips down to 1, he makes two eyes, one on the left and one on the right.

Wrong Answer

Connecting with Black 1 lets White play on the key point of 2. Black is left with one eye and a dead group.

Problem 129

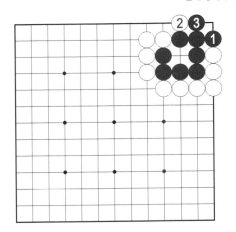 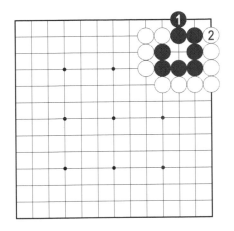

Correct Answer

Black 1 is the key move. If White 2, Black makes two eyes with 3, so his group is alive.

Wrong Answer

Black 1 lets White move into the corner with 2. Black can no longer make two eyes, so he is dead.

Problem 130

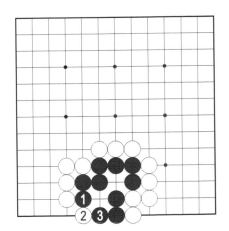 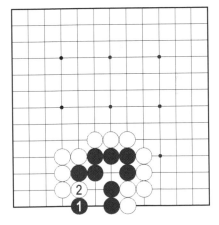

Correct Answer

Black 1 is the key point. If White 2, Black gets two eyes with 3 and his group is alive.

Wrong Answer

Black 1 lets White play 2. This leaves Black with only one eye and a dead group.

Answers to Problems 131 and 132

Problem 131

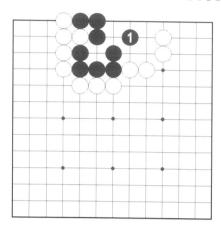

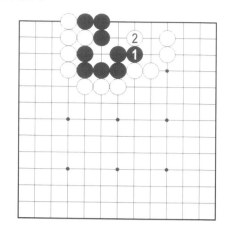

Correct Answer
Expanding Black's eye space with 1 gives him two eyes and a living group.

Wrong Answer
Black 1 lets White play on the key point of 2. Black can no longer make two eyes, so he is dead.

Problem 132

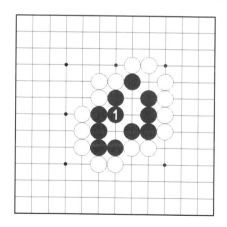

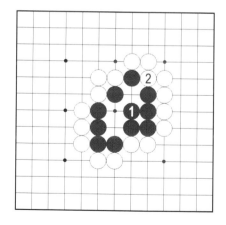

Correct Answer
Black 1 is the key point. White can't destroy Black's eyes, so he is alive.

Wrong Answer
If Black plays 1, White 2 destroys Black's second eye, so he is dead.

Problem 133

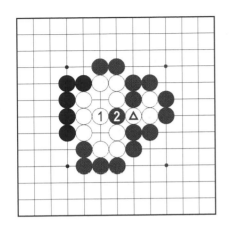

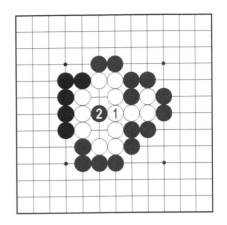

Correct Answer

White 1 makes two eyes above and below. If Black captures with 2, White recaptures with 3 (at the marked stone).

Wrong Answer

White 1 lets Black play on the key point of 2. White can no longer make two eyes, so his group is dead.

Problem 134

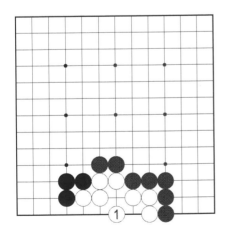

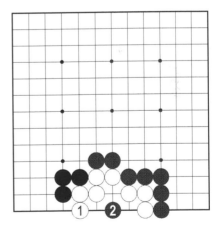

Correct Answer

White 1 is the key point. White's group now has two distinct eyes and can't be killed.

Wrong Answer

If White expands his eye space with 1, Black plays on the key point of 2, destroying White's eyes, thereby killing him.

Problem 135

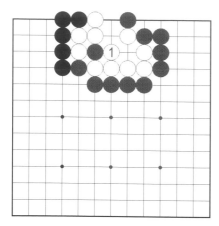

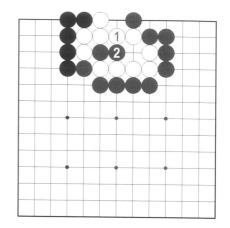

Correct Answer

Capturing with White 1 is the key move. White now has two distinct eyes and can't be killed.

Wrong Answer

White 1 lets Black play on the key point of 2. White is reduced to one eye, so he is dead.

Problem 136

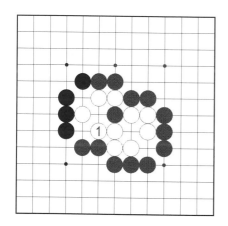

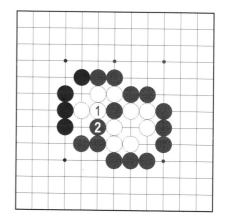

Correct Answer

White 1 is the key point. White has two distinct eyes and can't be killed.

Wrong Answer

If White captures a stone with 1, Black plays on the key point of 2, leaving White with only one eye, so he is dead.

Problem 137

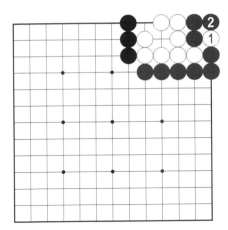

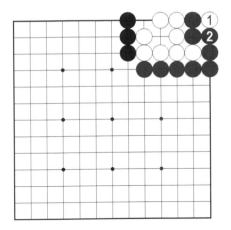

Correct Answer	*Wrong Answer*
White 1 sets up a snapback. If Black captures with 2, White 3 (at 1) captures three stones and White has two eyes.	If White plays 1, Black captures with 2 and White is left with only one eye.

Problem 138

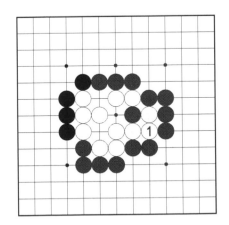

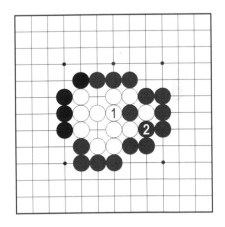

Correct Answer	*Wrong Answer*
White 1 is the key point. White now has two distinct eyes and his group can't be killed.	If White captures a stone with 1, Black 2 leaves White with only one real eye, so his group is dead.

Problem 139

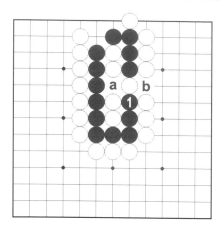 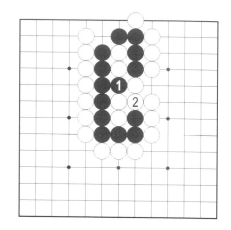

Correct Answer

Black 1 leaves two groups of two stones in atari and all four can be captured. If White 'a', Black 'b'; if White 'b', Black 'a'.

Wrong Answer

Black 1 lets White connect with 2, thereby saving two of his stones. Black is left with only one eye, so he is dead.

Problem 140

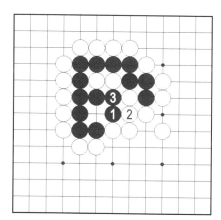 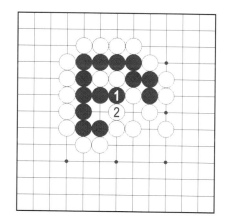

Correct Answer

Black 1 is the is the key move. After White connects with 2, Black captures with 3, leaving him with two eyes.

Wrong Answer

Capturing two stones with Black 1 lets White play on the key point of 2. Black is left with only one eye, so he is dead.

Problem 141

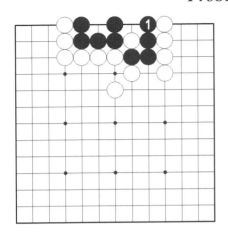 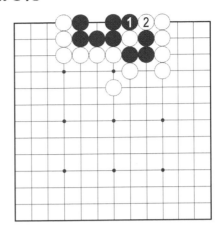

Correct Answer

Black 1 is the key point. Black now has two distinct eyes and can't be killed.

Wrong Answer

If Black captures a stone with 1, White plays on the key point of 2 and Black is left with only one eye.

Problem 142

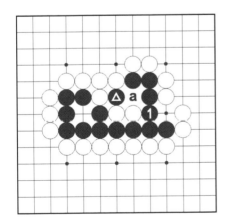 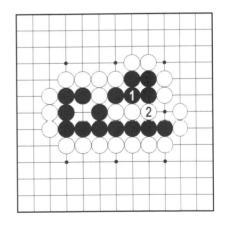

Correct Answer

Black 1 sets up a snapback. If White 'a' next, Black captures three stones at the marked stone and Black has two eyes.

Wrong Answer

Black puts himself into atari with 1, enabling White to capture five stones with 2. Black's group is dead.

Problem 143

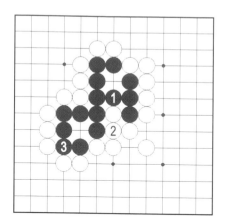

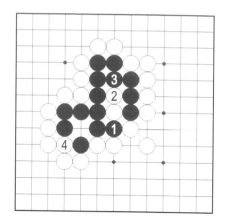

Correct Answer

Black 1 threatens to capture at 2. If White 2, Black makes a second eye with 3. If White plays 2 at 3, Black captures at 2.

Wrong Answer

If Black plays 1, White ataries with 2, then destroys White's second eye with 4. Black is dead.

Problem 144

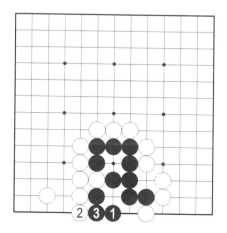

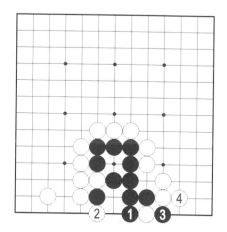

Correct Answer

Black 1 is the key point. There is no way that White can destroy Black's second eye. If White 2, Black 3.

Wrong Answer

If Black plays 1, White ataries with 2. Even though Black can capture a stone with 3, it is not an eye, so his group is dead.

Problem 145

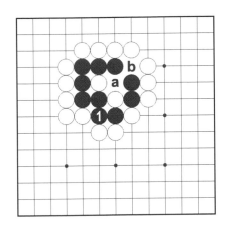

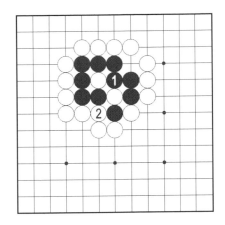

Correct Answer

If Black 1, White can't play at 'a' because it is an illegal move. If White 'b', Black captures at 'a' and gets two eyes.

Wrong Answer

Capturing two stones with Black 1 lets White destroy one of Black's eyes with 2, so Black's group is dead.

Problem 146

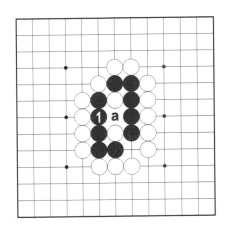

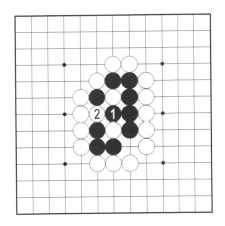

Correct Answer

If Black 1, White can't play at 'a' because it is an illegal move, so Black can eventually capture them and make two eyes.

Wrong Answer

Capturing two stones with Black 1 lets White destroy one of Black's eyes with 2, so Black's group is dead.

Problem 147

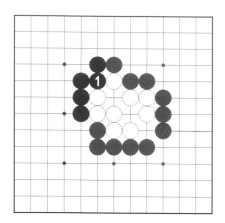

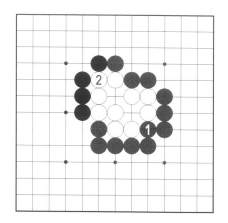

Correct Answer

The atari of Black 1 creates a false eye. White now has only one real eye, so his group is dead.

Wrong Answer

If Black plays 1, White 2 gives his group a second eye, so this group can never be killed.

Problem 148

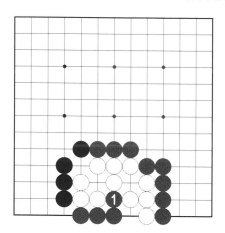

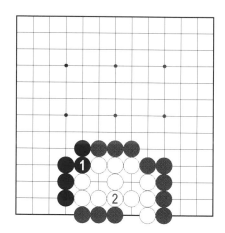

Correct Answer

If Black plays 1, the eye on the right become a false one, so White is dead.

Wrong Answer

Black 1 allows White to play 2, the key point to form two perfect eyes, so his group can never be killed.

Problem 149

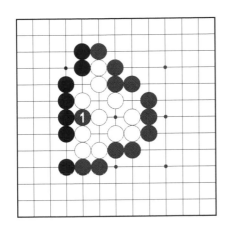

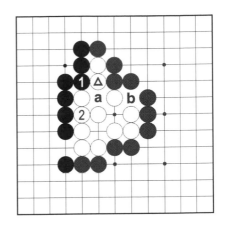

Correct Answer

Black 1 is the key point. The only real eye White has is the one on the right, so White is dead.

Wrong Answer

Black 1 lets White make two eyes with 2. If Black captures at 'a', White recaptures at the marked stone if Black plays at 'b'.

Problem 150

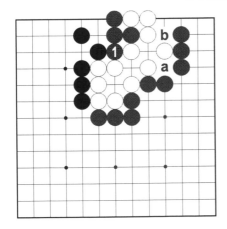

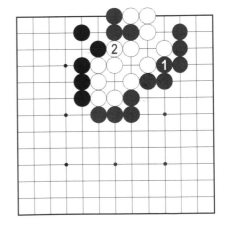

Correct Answer

Black 1 is the key point. The only eye White has is the one below. White is dead. If White 'a', Black 'b'; if White 'b', Black 'a'.

Wrong Answer

Black 1 lets White play on the key point of 2, making two eyes, so his group can never be killed.

Problem 151

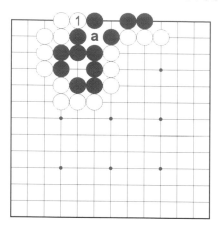

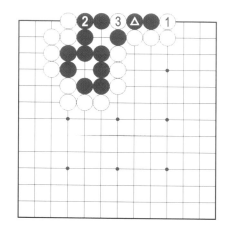

Correct Answer

White 1 is the key point. It makes the eye at 'a' a false one. Black has only one real eye, so he is dead.

Wrong Answer

The atari of White 1 lets Black connect with 2. If White 3, Black recaptures at the marked stone and his group is alive.

Problem 152

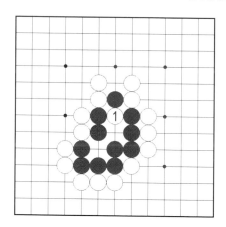

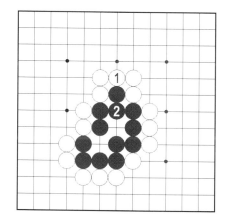

Correct Answer

Throwing in a stone with White 1 is the key move to create a false eye, so Black is dead.

Wrong Answer

The atari of White 1 lets Black play on the key point of 2, making two eyes, so his group can never be killed.

Problem 153

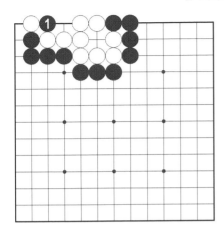 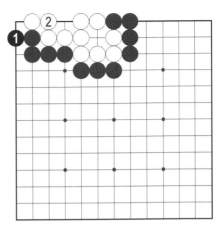

Correct Answer

Sacrificing a stone with Black 1 leaves White with a false eye, so his group is dead.

Wrong Answer

Making any other move, such as Black 1, lets White make a second eye with 2, so White's group is now alive.

Problem 154

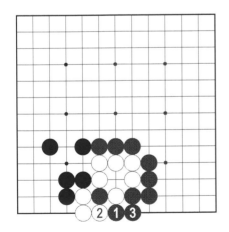 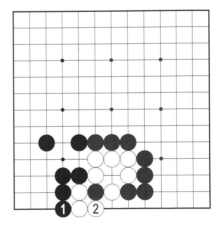

Correct Answer

The atari of Black 1 is the is the key move. After the exchange of 2 for Black 3, White is left with a false eye above 2.

Wrong Answer

If Black descends to 1, White lives by capturing a stone with 2, making a second eye and life.

Problem 155

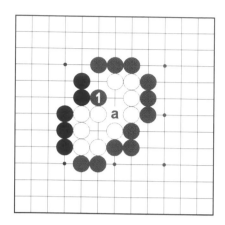

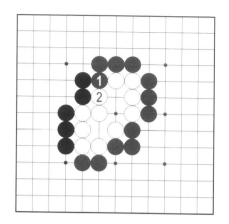

Correct Answer

Black 1 is the key point that creates a false eye at 'a'. White now has only one eye.

Wrong Answer

If Black plays 1, White makes two eyes with 2, securing life for his group.

Problem 156

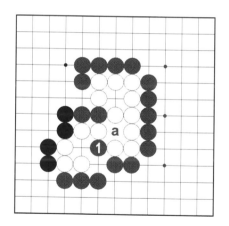

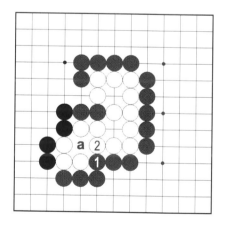

Correct Answer

Black 1 makes the white eye at 'a' a false one, so White is dead.

Wrong Answer

The atari of Black 1 lets White connect on the key point of 2. Even though Black can capture three stones with 'a', White has lived with the main body of his group.

Problem 157

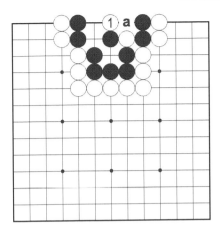

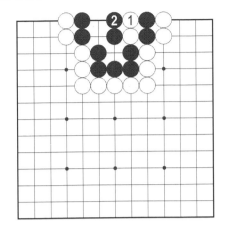

Correct Answer

White 1 is the key point. Capturing with Black 'a' is futile because of a snapback, so Black's group is dead.

Wrong Answer

If White captures two stones with 1, Black plays 2 and his remaining stones have two eyes. White has failed.

Problem 158

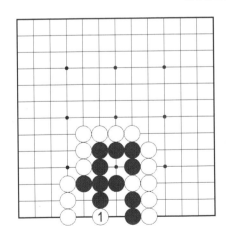

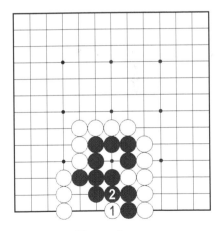

Correct Answer

White 1 is the key point. No matter how Black plays, he can't make another eye, so his group is dead.

Wrong Answer

If White ataries with 1, Black 2 traps the invading stone, so Black gets a second eye for his group.

Problem 159

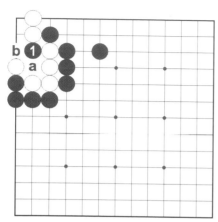
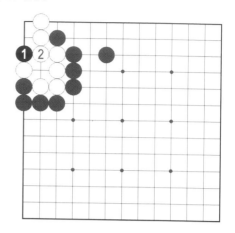

Correct Answer

Black 1 is the key move that puts four white stones into atari. If White 'a', Black captures at 'b'. The white stones are dead.

Wrong Answer

If Black ataries with 1, White can start a ko with 2. Since White is not unconditionally dead, Black has failed.

Problem 160

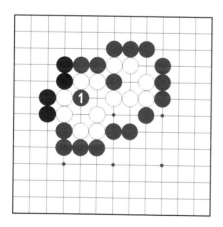
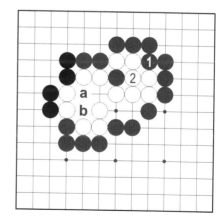

Correct Answer

The double atari of Black 1 is the only move. All the white stones will die.

Wrong Answer

If Black 1, White captures with 2. The atari of Black 'a' is now ineffective. White connects at 'b' and suffers no damage.

Problem 161

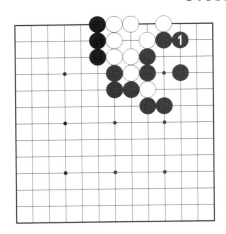

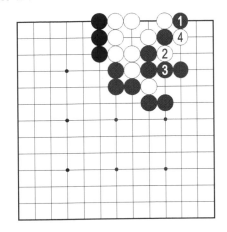

Correct Answer

Extending to Black 1 is the best move. White's eye on the first line is false, so his group is dead.

Wrong Answer

If Black ataries with 1, White 2 and 4 capture a stone and make an eye. If Black 1 at 2, White plays at 4 and his group is alive.

Problem 162

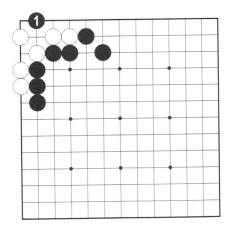

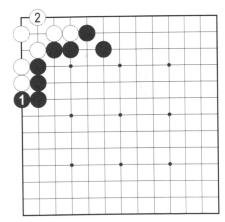

Correct Answer

Black 1 is the key point. White is dead, as he can't make two eyes.

Wrong Answer

If Black plays 1, White lives by playing 2. Only capturing the two stones in atari would be a failure for Black.

Problem 163

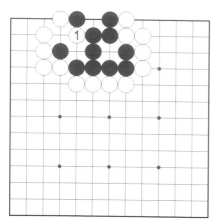

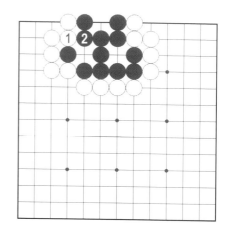

Correct Answer

White 1 makes Black's eye at the top a false one, so Black is dead.

Wrong Answer

If White plays 1, Black gets two eyes and a living group by connecting with 2.

Problem 164

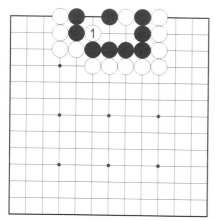

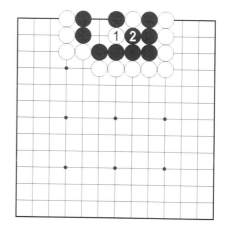

Correct Answer

White 1 is the key point. This move captures more than two stones: it kills the whole black group.

Wrong Answer

If White ataries with 1, Black will capture with 2 and all of his stones are alive.

Problem 165

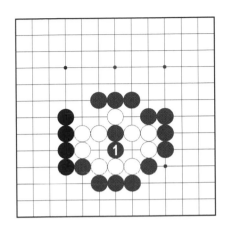

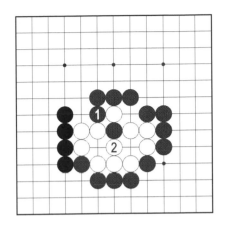

Correct Answer

By sacrificing two stones with 1, Black reduces White's group to one eye, thereby killing it.

Wrong Answer

If Black ataries with 1, White captures a stone with 2, making two eyes and life for his group.

Problem 166

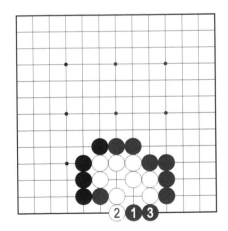

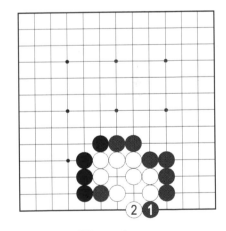

Correct Answer

Black 1 is the key point. When Black links up with 3, White has only one eye, so he is dead.

Wrong Answer

If Black plays a hane with 1, White makes two eyes with 2, so his group is alive.

Problem 167

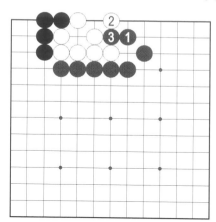 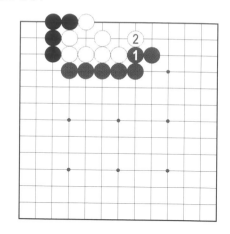

Correct Answer

Black 1 is the only move. No matter how White answers, he can't make two eyes. If White 2 at 3, Black will play at 2.

Wrong Answer

If Black plays 1, White lives with 2. Black 1 in the correct answer is the only move that kills White.

Problem 168

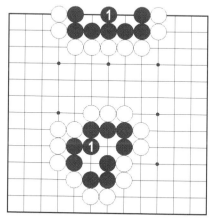 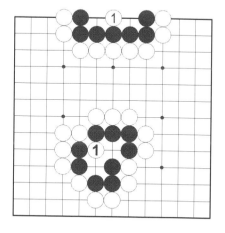

Correct Answer

Black gets two eyes and life both at the top and bottom positions if he plays 1.

If White Plays First

If it's White turn, he can play 1 both at the top and bottom positions and kill the black groups.

Problem 169

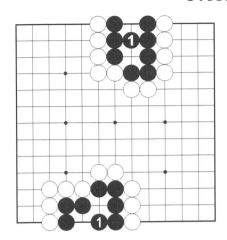

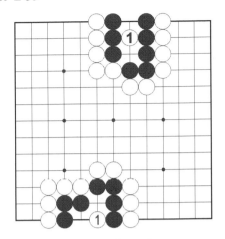

Correct Answer
If Black plays 1 at the top and bottom positions, he makes two eyes and lives.

If White Plays First
If it's White's turn, White 1 in the top and bottom positions kills the black groups.

Problem 170

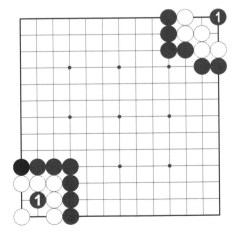

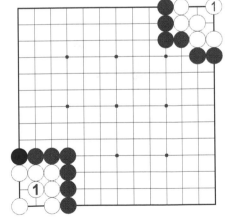

Correct Answer
If Black plays 1 at the top and bottom positions, White can't make two eyes, so he dies.

If White Plays First
If it's White's turn, he can make two eyes and live by playing 1.

Problem 171

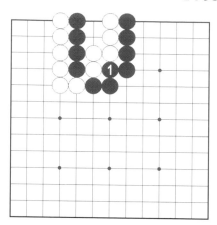

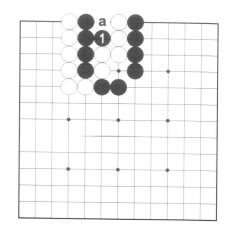

Correct Answer

Black 1 is the only move. The four black stones and the five white stones both live in a seki.

Wrong Answer

Black 1 puts five of his stones into atari, so White can capture them by playing at 'a'. Black has failed.

Problem 172

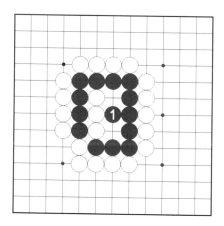

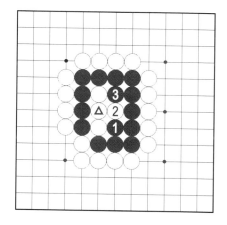

Correct Answer

Black 1 creates a seki. If White breaks the seki by sacrificing four stones, Black will capture and get a living four-space eye.

If White Plays First

If Black 1, White 2 sacrifices four stones. If Black captures with 3, White 4 at the marked stone leaves Black with one eye.

Problem 173

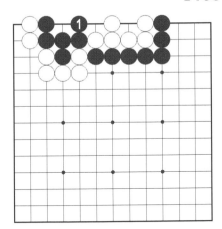 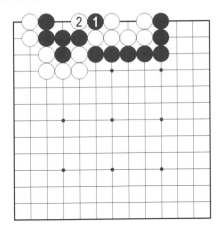

Correct Answer

Making an eye with Black 1 is the only move. Both sides have one eye and share a neutral point, so the position is a seki.

Wrong Answer

If Black plays 1, White 2 captures a stone and puts five stones into atari.

Problem 174

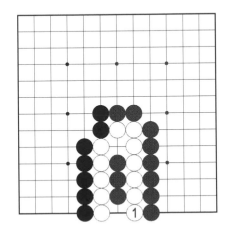 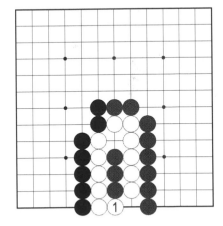

Correct Answer

White 1 is the only move. White has no way to capture the three black stones, so he must settle for a seki.

Wrong Answer

If White tries to capture the black stones with the atari of 1, he ends up with a dead three-space eye.

Problem 175

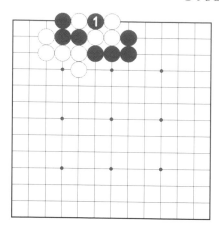 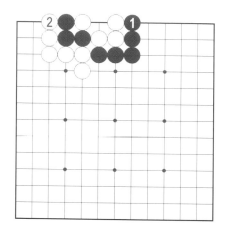

Correct Answer

The only way Black can save his three stones at the top is to start a ko with 1. If he has more ko threats, he will win the ko.

Wrong Answer

If Black ataries with 1, White will capture three stones with 2.

Problem 176

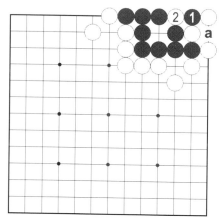 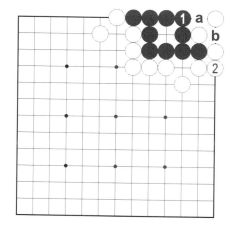

Correct Answer

Black should start a ko by sacrificing a stone with 1. Black can resolve the ko by capturing at 'a'.

Wrong Answer

If Black connects with 1, White will connect with 2. Black's group has only one eye. If Black 'a', White 'b'.

Problem 177

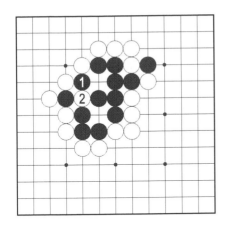 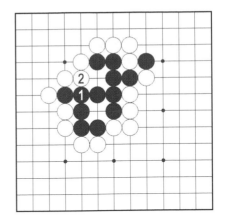

Correct Answer

Black 1 is the only way to create a ko. White starts the ko by capturing with 2 and Black must make a ko threat.

Wrong Answer

If Black connects with 1, White will play 2, leaving Black with only one eye. Black is now unconditionally dead.

Problem 178

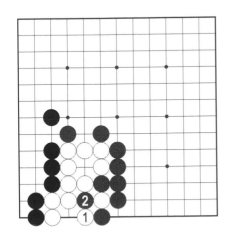 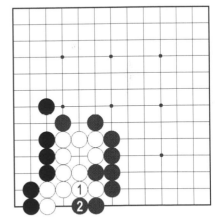

Correct Answer

White 1 is the only move that creates a ko. Black starts the ko with 2 and White must make a ko threat.

Wrong Answer

If White connects with 1, Black will play 2, leaving White with only one eye. White is now unconditionally dead.

Problem 179

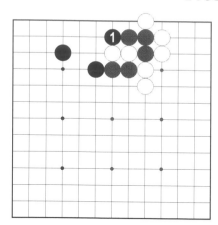

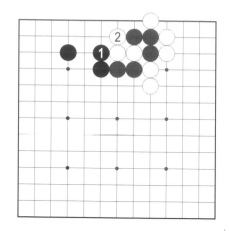

Correct Answer

The atari of Black 1 is the only move. The two white stones can't escape.

Wrong Answer

If Black ataries from the left with 1, White 2 will capture three stones.

Problem 180

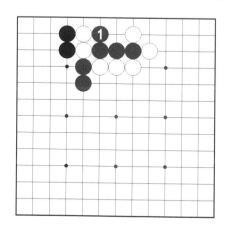

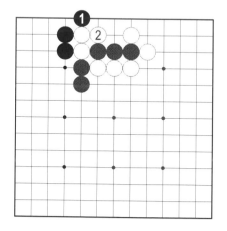

Correct Answer

Black 1 is the only move. White's two stones can't avoid capture.

Wrong Answer

If Black ataries on the first line with 1, White 2 captures three stones.

Problem 181

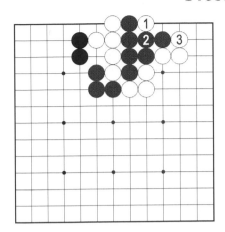 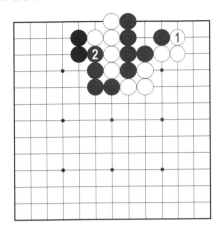

Correct Answer

The atari of White 1, followed by White 3, is the correct move. The seven black stones can't avoid capture.

Wrong Answer

If White plays 1, Black will atari with 2 and capture five stones on the next move.

Problem 182

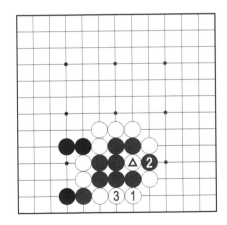 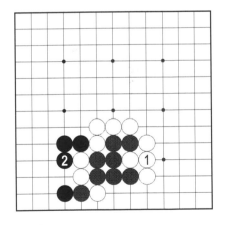

Correct Answer

White 1, followed by White 3, sets up an *oiotoshi*. If Black connects at the marked stone, he will still be in atari.

Wrong Answer

If White connects with 1, Black will play 2 and capture two stones on the next move.

Problem 183

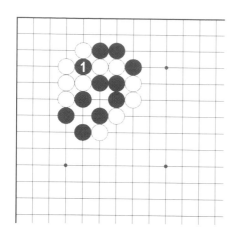

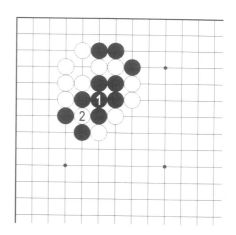

Correct Answer

Black should capture two stones with 1. Even if White recaptures, Black will no longer be in atari.

Wrong Answer

If Black connects with 1, his stones are still in atari and White 2 will capture six stones. This is a disaster for Black.

Problem 184

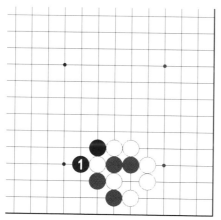

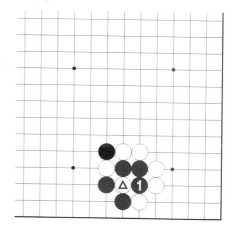

Correct Answer

Black should capture the stone on the outside with 1.

Wrong Answer

If Black captures with 1, White will play 2 at the marked stone and capture three stones in a snapback.

Problem 185

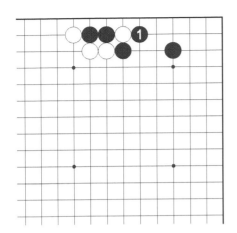

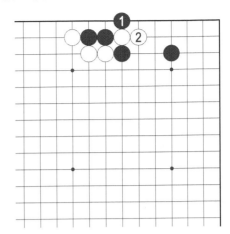

Correct Answer

If Black ataries with 1, the isolated white stone on the second line can't escape.

Wrong Answer

If Black ataries with 1, White's stone can't be captured after White 2. Instead, the three black stones at the top will be captured.

Problem 186

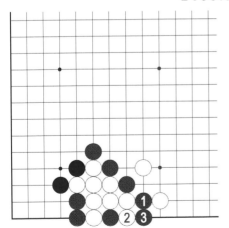

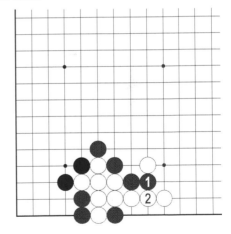

Correct Answer

After Black ataries with 1 and 3, the eight white stones will be captured on the next move.

Wrong Answer

Black 1 here fails. When White connects with 2, his stones at the bottom are safe and can no longer be captured.

Problem 187

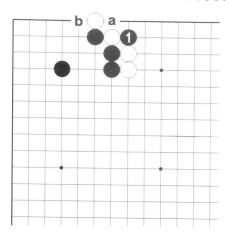

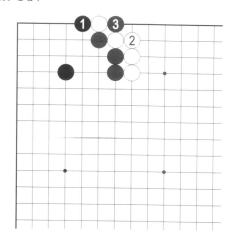

Correct Answer

Black should atari with 1. The white stone in atari can't escape. If White 'a', Black ataries again at 'b'.

Wrong Answer

If Black ataries with 1, White connects at 2. Black has captured a stone, but this result is inferior to the correct answer.

Problem 188

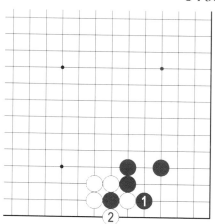

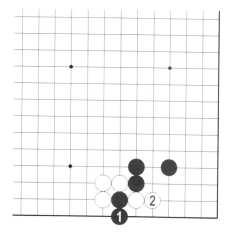

Correct Answer

Even though he loses a stone, Black 1 is the best move.

Wrong Answer

Descending to Black 1 fails. When White extends to 2, Black's two stones at the bottom are dead.

Problem 189

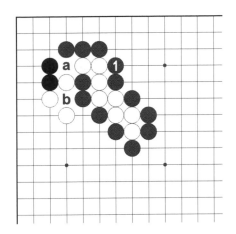 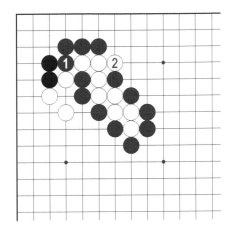

Correct Answer

If Black ataries with 1, White's stones can't escape. If White 'a', Black captures at 'b'.

Wrong Answer

If Black ataries with 1, White can escape into the open with his eight stones by playing 2.

Problem 190

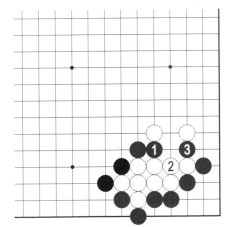 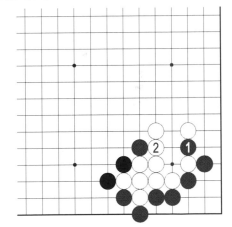

Correct Answer

Black should atari with 1. Connecting with 2 doesn't help White. Black 3 captures nine stones.

Wrong Answer

If Black ataries with 1, White can link up to his stone on the outside by connecting at 2.

Problem 191

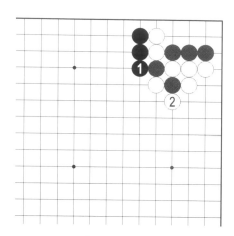

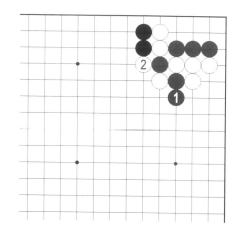

Correct Answer

Black has no choice but to connect with 1. After White captures with 2, Black's territory at the top is intact.

Wrong Answer

If Black saves his other stone with 1, White captures with 2 and Black's stones are split into three weak groups.

Problem 192

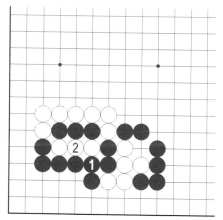

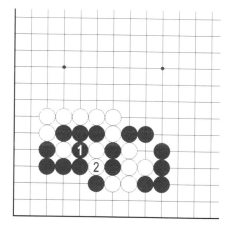

Correct Answer

Black should play 1, saving two stones and sacrificing three. In this way, he kills the five white stones on the right.

Wrong Answer

If Black plays 1, rescuing three stones, White captures two stones with 2 and all of his stones are linked up.

Problem 193

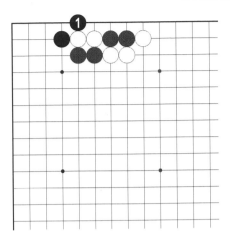

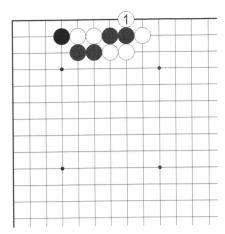

Correct Answer

If Black ataries with 1, he will capture two stones.

If White Plays First

If it were White's turn, he would atari with 1 and capture two stones.

Problem 194

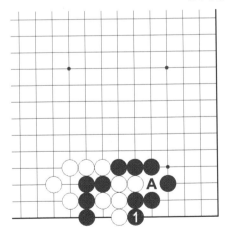

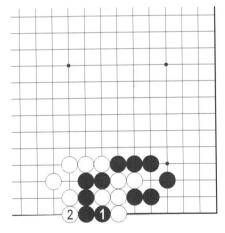

Correct Answer

Either Black 1 or Black A will capture five white stones.

Wrong Answer

It is usually a bad move to fill an inside liberty in a capturing race. After Black 1, White 2 puts five stones into atari.

Problem 195

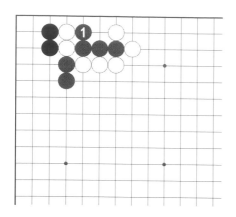

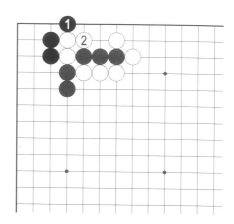

Correct Answer

Black 1 captures two white stones.

If White Plays First

If Black ataries from below with 1, White 2 will capture three stones.

Problem 196

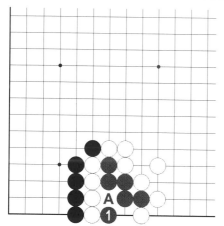

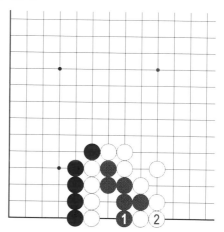

Correct Answer

Putting the four white stones into atari with Black 1 or A is the right move. Black can capture these stones on the next move.

Wrong Answer

If Black ataries on the right with 1, he fails. White connects with 2 and the position becomes a seki.

Problem 197

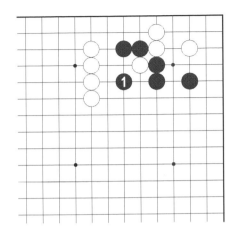

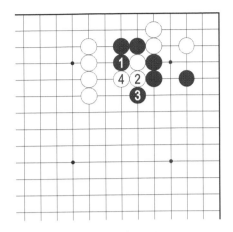

Correct Answer

Black can capture a stone in a net when he plays 1. White's stone can't escape and will be captured.

If White Plays First

Black 1 fails. White escapes with 2 and 4.

Problem 198

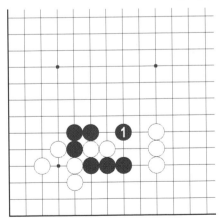

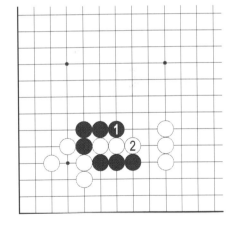

Correct Answer

Black 1 captures two stones in a net. These stones can't escape and will be captured.

Wrong Answer

Black 1 fails. White extends 2 and his stones can't be captured.

Problem 199

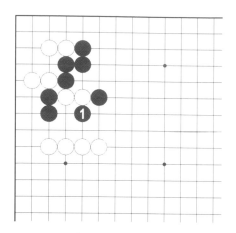

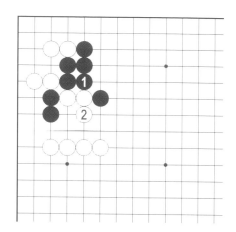

Correct Answer

Black 1 captures two stones. White has no way to rescue them.

Wrong Answer

Black 1 fails. White escape by extending to 2.

Problem 200

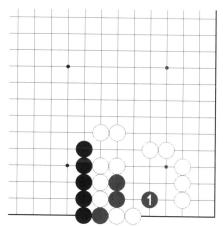

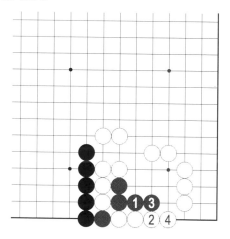

Correct Answer

Black 1 is an example of a net played at the edge of the board. The two white stones can't escape.

Wrong Answer

The atari of Black 1 fails. White runs away and links up with his other stones with the moves to 4.

Problem 201

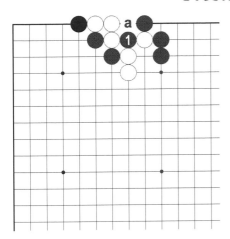

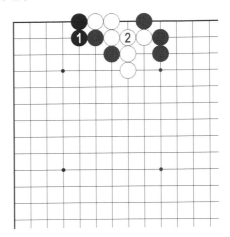

Correct Answer

Black 1 captures the three white stones at the top. If White captures at 'a', Black 1 recaptures four stones in a snapback.

Wrong Answer

If Black connects at 1, he fails. White connects with 2 and his stones can't be captured.

Problem 202

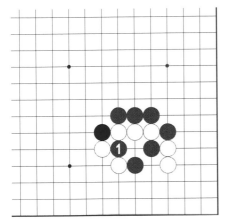

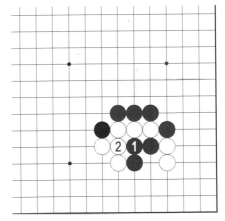

Correct Answer

Black can capture three stones by throwing in a stone with 1. If White captures, Black recaptures in a snapback.

Wrong Answer

The atari of Black 1 fails. White connects with 2 and his stones are safe.

Problem 203

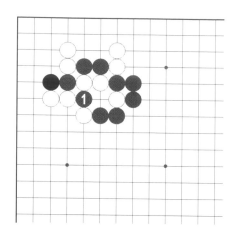

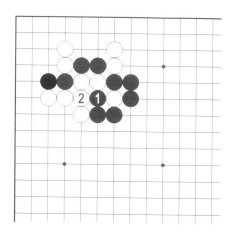

Correct Answer
Black 1 sets up a snapback and captures three stones.

Wrong Answer
Black 1 captures a stone, but it lets White save his other two by connecting with 2. Black has failed.

Problem 204

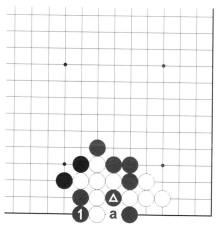

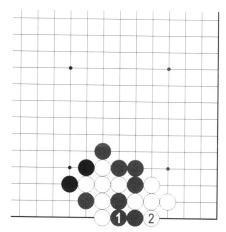

Correct Answer
Black 1 sets up a snapback and six white stones can't escape. If White captures at 'a', Black recaptures at the marked stone.

Wrong Answer
The atari of Black 1 fails. White 2 captures three stones and all of White's stones are safe.

Problem 205

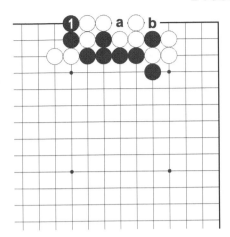

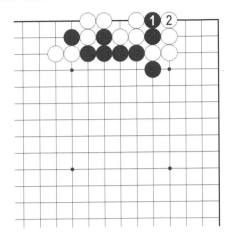

Correct Answer

Black ataries with 1. If White connects at 'a', he will still be in atari (*oiotoshi*) and Black will capture six stones with 'b'.

Wrong Answer

If Black ataries with 1, White captures two stones with 2 and all of White's stones are safe.

Problem 206

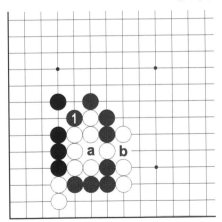

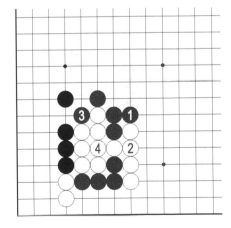

Correct Answer

Black 1 puts six stones into atari. If White connects 'a', his stones will still be in atari (*oiotoshi*), so Black can capture at 'b'.

Wrong Answer

Black 1 gives White time to connect with 2. If Black now ataries with 3, White connects with 4 and all his stones are safe.

Problem 207

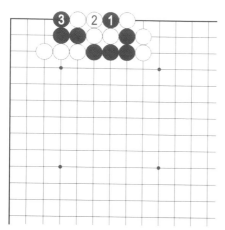

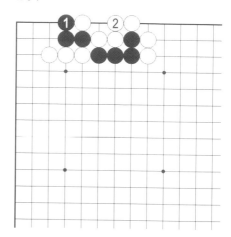

Correct Answer

Black sacrifices a stone with 1, then ataries with 3. White can't connect at 1, as he would still be in atari, so he loses four stones.

Wrong Answer

If Black first plays 1, he fails. White connects with 2 and his stones are safe, but Black's three stones on the left are dead.

Problem 208

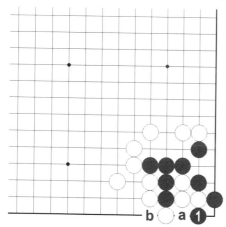

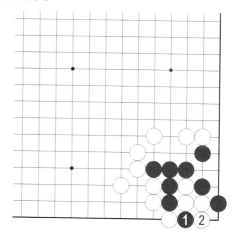

Correct Answer

Black 1 capture the three stones in the corner. If White resists by connecting at 'a', Black captures at 'b'.

Wrong Answer

Sacrificing a stone with 1 fails. After White 2, Black has no follow-up move to capture White, so the black stones are dead.

Problem 209

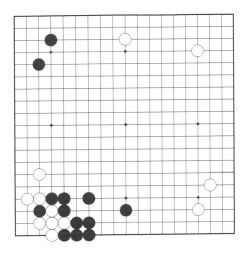

Correct Answer

White has profited more with the moves in the problem diagram. If you compare the diagram above with the one below, the difference should be clear.

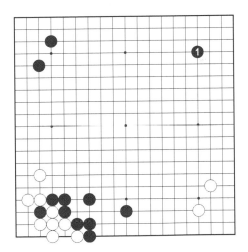

Reference Diagram

Occupying the empty corner with Black 1 is the most profitable move. Black's position is better by about 30 points than the diagram above.

Problem 210

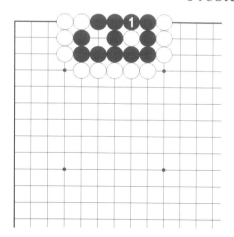

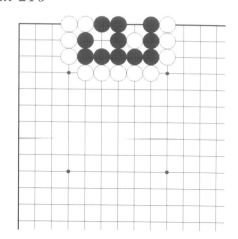

Black 1 is bad.

Black 1 is a bad move. It is completely unnecessary, as Black is unconditionally alive.

Reference Diagram

Black should leave the situation as it is. By playing 1 in the preceding diagram, he loses one point of territory.

Problem 211

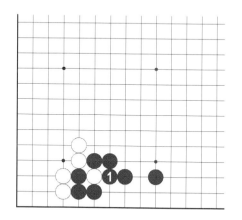

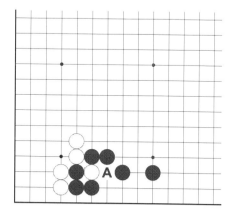

Black 1 is bad.

Black 1 is a bad move. It is unnecessary for Black to play this move.

Reference Diagram

Even if White tries to escape by playing at A, his stones are still in atari. Black still has no need to answer.

Problem 212

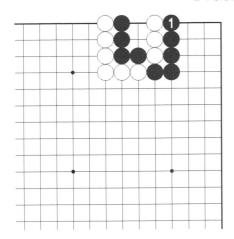

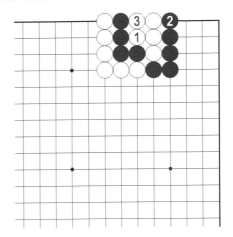

Correct Answer

If Black plays 1, a seki results between the four black and the three white stones.

If White Plays First

If it were White's turn, he could capture four stones with 1 and 3.

Problem 213

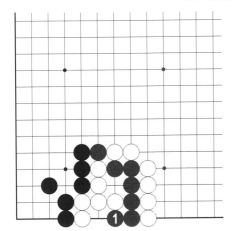

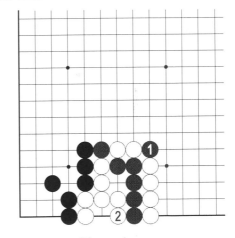

Correct Answer

If Black plays 1, a seki results between the six white stones and the six black ones.

Wrong Answer

If Black makes any other move, such as the cut of 1, White ataries with 2 and captures five stones.

Problem 214

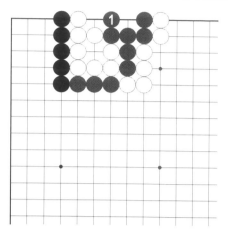

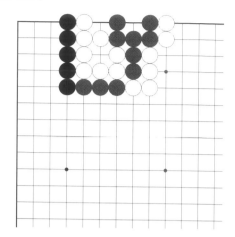

Correct Answer

Black 1 creates a seki between the eight white stones on the left and seven black stones on the right.

Reference Diagram

In this seki, both sides have an eye, but these eyes are not counted as territory.

Problem 215

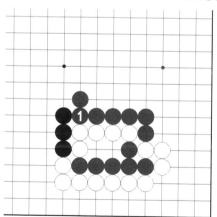

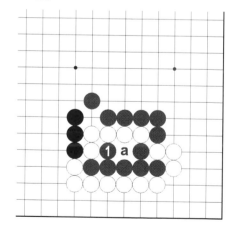

Correct Answer

Black 1 results in a seki between the five white stones and the six black ones.

Wrong Answer

Black 1 fails. The black stones are dead as they stand. If necessary, White can capture them by playing at 'a'.

Problem 216

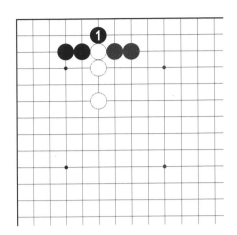

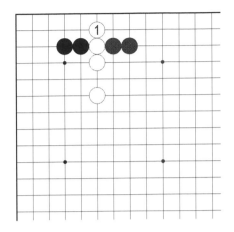

Correct Answer

If Black plays 1, the black stones on the left and right are linked up and White can't separate them.

If White Plays First

If it were White's turn, he would descend to 1 and the black stones would be split into two groups.

Problem 217

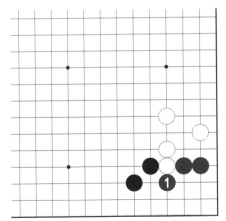

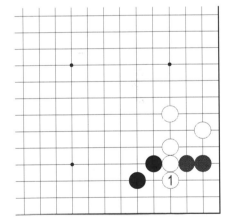

Correct Answer

By playing 1, Black links up his stones on the left and right.

If White Plays First

If it were White's turn, he would play 1 and the black stones would be split into two groups.

Problem 218

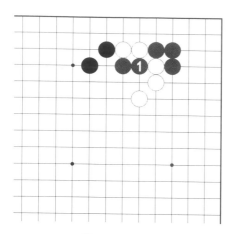

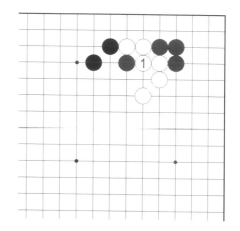

Correct Answer

If Black plays 1, the two white stones above are separated from the ones below and they will be captured.

If White Plays First

If it were White's turn, he would connect with 1. All of White's stones are now linked up and Black's are separated.

Problem 219

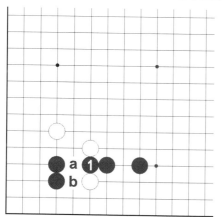

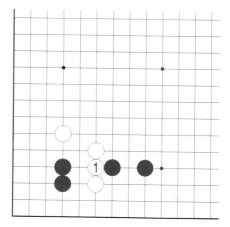

Correct Answer

By playing 1, Black can link up his two groups. If White resists with 'a', Black ataries with 'b'.

If White Plays First

If it were White's turn, he would connect with 1. White's stones are now strong and Black must struggle to live in the corner.

Problem 220

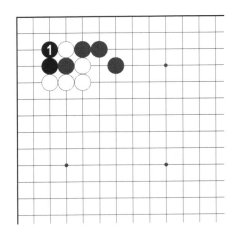

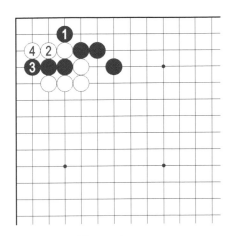

Correct Answer

If Black ataries with 1, the white stone can't avoid capture and Black's stones will link up into one group.

Wrong Answer

If Black ataries with 1, White 2 to 4 can be expected. The black stones can't avoid capture.

Problem 221

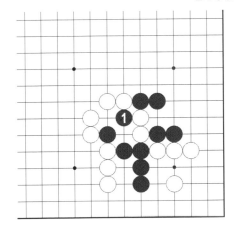

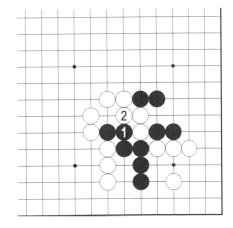

Correct Answer

Black 1 captures two stones. Black's stones above and below are now linked up.

Wrong Answer

If Black connects with 1, White connects with 2 and the six black stones below are cut off from their allies above.

Problem 222

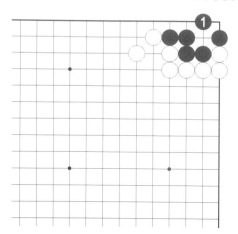

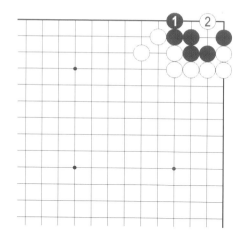

Correct Answer

If Black plays 1, he has two eyes, so his stones are alive.

Wrong Answer

If Black descends to 1, White plays 2 on the key point and reduces Black's group to one eye.

Problem 223

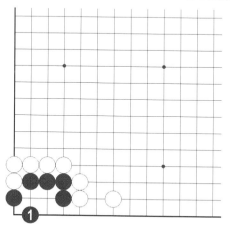

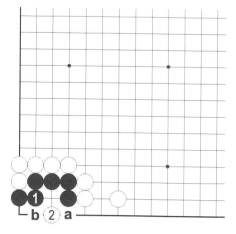

Correct Answer

If Black plays 1, his group gets two eyes and can't be killed.

Wrong Answer

In response to Black 1, White plays 2. Black's group can no longer make two eyes, so it is dead. If Black 'a', White 'b'.

Problem 224

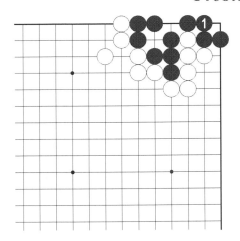 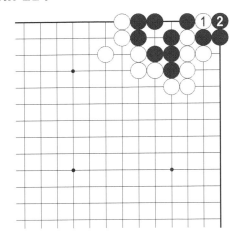

Correct Answer

If Black connects at 1, his group has two eyes, so it is alive.

If White Plays First

If it were White's turn, he would sacrifice a stone with 1. After 2, Black's two eyes on the edge are false, so he dies.

Problem 225

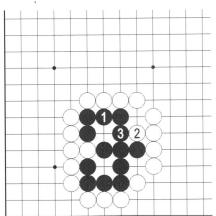 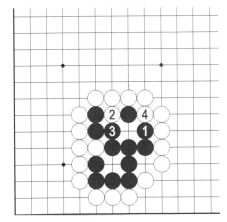

Correct Answer

If Black plays 1, he can play 3 in response to White's only threat at 2. Black now has two eyes, so he is alive.

Wrong Answer

If Black plays 1, White 2 and 4 reduce the eye at the top to a false one, so Black is dead.

Problem 226

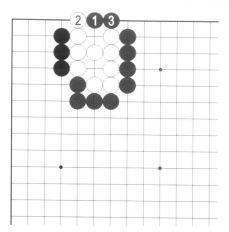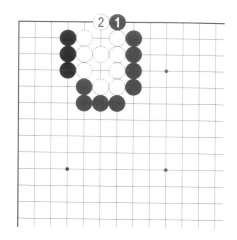

Correct Answer

If Black plays 1, White's group can't make two eyes, so it is dead. If White plays 2 at 3, Black plays at 2.

Wrong Answer

If Black plays a hane with 1, he fails. White's group gets two eyes when he plays 2.

Problem 227

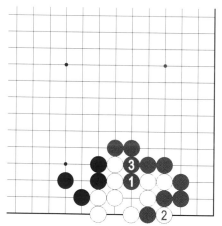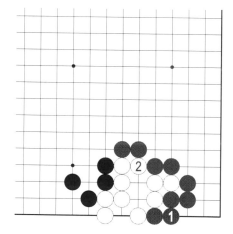

Correct Answer

Black 1 and 3 kill White's group. Even though White has captured a black stone, he has only made a false eye.

Wrong Answer

If Black connects with 1, White gets two eyes when he plays 2. His group is now alive.

Problem 228

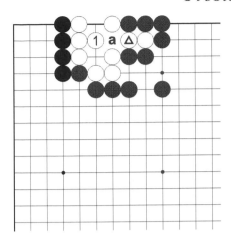

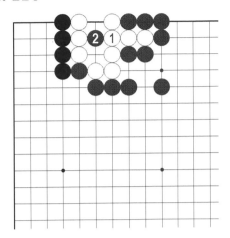

Correct Answer

If White plays 1, his group is alive. If Black captures at 'a', White recaptures at the marked stone.

Wrong Answer

If White plays any other move, such as 1, Black will play on the key point of 2 and White is dead.

Problem 229

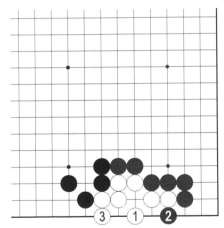

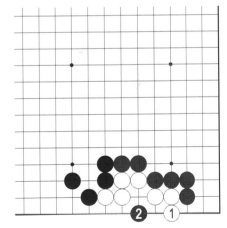

Correct Answer

If White plays 1, his group is alive. If Black 2, White 3; if Black 2 at 3, White 2. Either way, White's group gets two eyes.

Wrong Answer

If White plays any other move, such as 1, Black will play on the key point of 2 and White is dead.

Problem 230

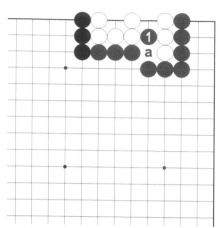
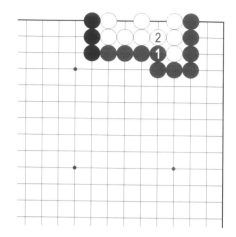

Correct Answer

If Black plays 1, White's group can't make two eyes. White can't play at 'a' because his stones are short of liberties.

Wrong Answer

If Black plays 1, White makes two eyes with 2 and his group is alive.

Problem 231

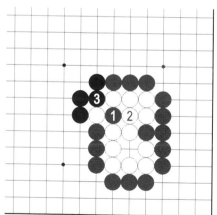
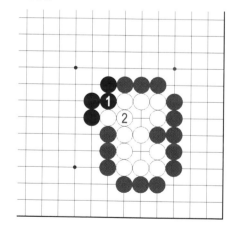

Correct Answer

Black 1 is the key point. After White 2, Black 3 makes the point 1 a false eye. If White 2 at 3, Black captures at 2.

Wrong Answer

Black 1 fails. White makes two eyes by connecting at 2.

Problem 232

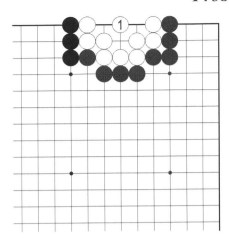

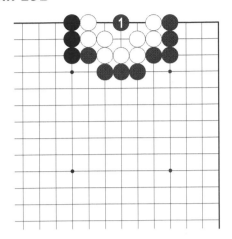

Correct Answer

White 1 is the key point. White's group has three eyes, so it is absolutely alive.

If Black Plays First

If it were Black's turn, he would reduce White's group to one eye by playing 1. White's group is dead.

Problem 233

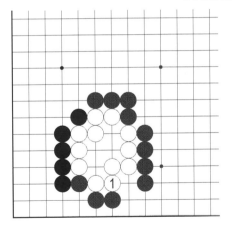

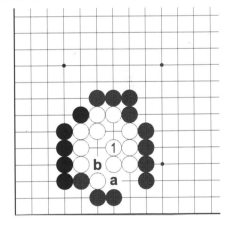

Correct Answer

White 1 is the key point. White's group now has a living four-space eye.

Inferior

White could also live by playing 1, but after Black exchanges 'a' for White 'b', he has only two points instead of four.

Problem 234

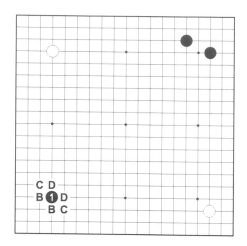

Correct Answer

Black 1, or any of the points from A to D, would be correct. It is usually advantageous to take an empty corner in the opening.

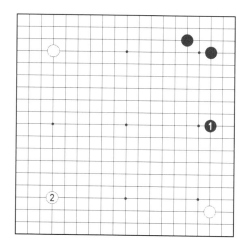

Wrong Answer

Black 1 is certainly a good strategic move, but playing in the empty corner is still better. After White plays 2, Black's position is inferior.

Problem 235

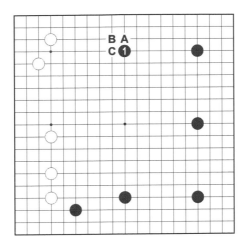

Correct Answer

In a position such as this, extending along the side is the usual way to play. Instead of Black 1, playing at A, B, or C would also be good.

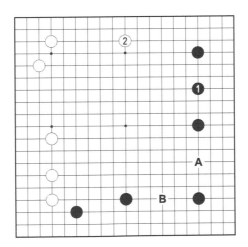

Wrong Answer

Playing Black 1 or at one of the points A or B would not be good. White would take a big strategic point on the side with 2 and he now has the advantage.

Problem 236

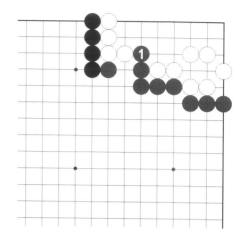

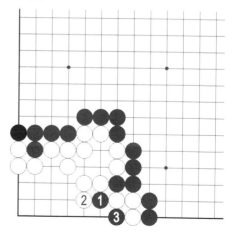

Correct Answer

White 1 seals off the territory at the top, securing 19 points of territory.

If Black Plays First

If it were Black's turn, he would invade with 1 and devastate White's territory at the top.

Problem 237

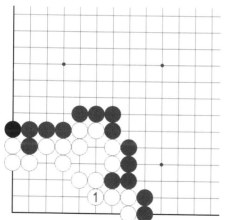

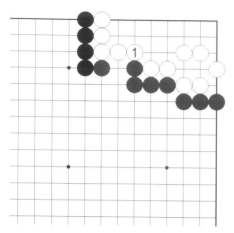

Correct Answer

White 1 defends the last defect in his position. This move secures 20 points of territory in the corner.

If Black Plays First

If it were Black's turn, he would capture three stones with 1 and 3. This would make a big dent in White's territory.

Problem 238

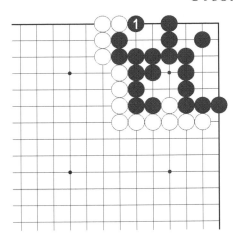

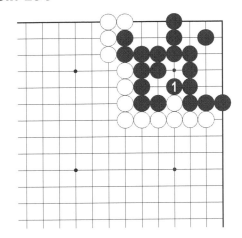

Correct Answer

Black 1 is the biggest move. It defends three points of territory This is where White would play if it were his turn.

Wrong Answer

Black 1 defends only two points instead of the three in the Correct Answer.

Problem 239

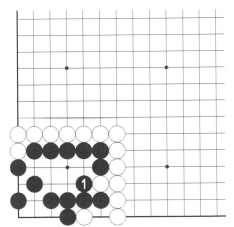

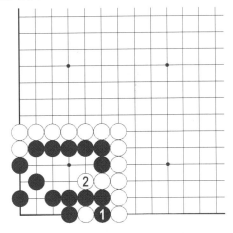

Correct Answer

Black 1 is the bigger point. It is worth three points.

Wrong Answer

Capturing a stone with Black 1 is worth only two points, whereas White 2 is worth three points.

Go Books from Kiseido

Introductory and General

K50: **Go — A Complete Introduction to the Game** by Cho Chikun
K40: **The Go Player's Almanac 2001** edited by Richard Bozulich
K30: **Japanese Prints and the World of Go** by William Pinckard and Kitagawa Akiko

Problem Books for Beginners

Graded Go Problems for Beginners by Kano Yoshinori
K46: Volumes 1, Introductory Problems (30-kyu to 25-kyu)
K47: Volumes 2, Elementary Problems (25-kyu to 20-kyu)
K48: Volumes 3, Intermediate Problems (20-kyu to 15-kyu)
K46: Volumes 4, Advanced Problems (15-kyu to 1-kyu)

Elementary Go Series

For more than 30 years, the Elementary Go Series has been the standard texts for go players who want to get a firm grasp of the fundamentals of go. Not only is the theory of go elaborated on, the reader is also given problems to show how these theoretical concepts are applied in actual games.

K10: Volume 1: **In the Beginning — The Opening in the Game of Go** by Ishigure Ikuro
K11: Volume 2: **38 Basic Joseki** by Kosugi Kiyoshi and James Davies
K12: Volume 3: **Tesuji** by James Davies
K13: Volume 4: **Life and Death** by James Davies
K14: Volume 5: **Attack and Defense** by Ishida Akira and James Davies
K15: Volume 6: **The Endgame** by Ogawa Tomoko and James Davies
K16: Volume 7: **Handicap Go** by Nagahara Yoshiaki and Richard Bozulich

Get Strong at Go Series

A series of problem books covering every phase of the game from the opening to the endgame. Each book contains 170 or more problems ranging in difficulty from elementary to advanced. Thus, they can be used by players ranging in strength from 20-kyu to dan-level. By studying go in this problem format, you will not only learn basic principles as to why moves are made but also train yourself in thinking through and analyzing positions. You will encounter a great many of the same or similar patterns that will arise in your own games. We guarantee that diligent study of this entire series will lay the foundation for becoming a truly strong player.

K51: Volume 1: **Get Strong at the Opening**
K52: Volume 2: **Get Strong at Joseki I**
K53: Volume 3: **Get Strong at Joseki II**
K54: Volume 4: **Get Strong at Joseki III**
K55: Volume 5: **Get Strong at Invading**
K56: Volume 6: **Get Strong at Tesuji**
K57: Volume 7: **Get Strong at the Endgame**
K58: Volume 8: **Get Strong at Life and Death**
K59: Volume 9: **Get Strong at Handicap Go**
K60: Volume 10: **Get Strong at Attacking**

Mastering the Basics

A series of books, especially written for high-kyu players, for mastering the basic techniques of go. Each book in this series consists of hundreds of problems designed to hammer home the fundamental concepts of go theory and technique. A thorough and patient study of this series is the fastest way to advance through the kyu ranks.

K71: Volume 1: **501 Opening Problems**, by Richard Bozulich and Rob van Zeijst
K72: Volume 2: **1001 Life-and-Death Problems**, by Richard Bozulich
K73: Volume 3: **Making Good Shape**, by Rob van Zeijst and Richard Bozulich
K74: Volume 4: **501 Tesuji Problems,** by Richard Bozulich
K75: Volume 5: **The Basics of Go Strategy,** by Richard Bozulich
K76: Volume 6: **All About Ko,** by Rob van Zeijst and Richard Bozulich
K77: Volume 7: **Attacking and Defending Moyos,** by van Zeijst and Bozulich
K78: Volume Eight: **Fight Like a Pro — The Secrets of Kiai**
      by Rob van Zeijst and Richard Bozulich
K79: Volume Nine: **An Encyclopedia of Go Principles** by Richard Bozulich
K80: Volume Ten: **Close Encounters with the Middle Game** by Michiel Eijkhout

Elementary Books

K02: Basic Techniques of Go, by Nagahara Yoshiaki and Haruyama Isamu
K28: Lessons in the Fundamentals of Go by Kageyama Toshiro
K36: Opening Theory Made Easy by Otake Hideo
K84: The Basics of Life and Death by Rob van Zeijst and Richard Bozulich
K85: A Survey of Basic Tesujis by Richard Bozulich

Advanced Books

Graded Go Problems for Dan Players
    K61: Volume 1 — 300 Life and Death Problems 5-kyu to 3-dan
    K62: Volume 2 — 300 Tesuji Problems 5-kyu to 3-dan
    K63: Volume 3 — 300 Joseki Problems 1-dan to 3-dan
    K64: Volume 4 — 300 Life and Death Problems 4-dan to 7-dan
    K65: Volume 5 — 300 Tesuji Problems 4-dan to 7-dan
    K66: Volume 6 — 300 Joseki Problems 4-dan to 7-dan
    K67: Volume 7 — Opening and Middle Game Problems 1-dan to 7-dan

K81: A Dictionary of Modern Fuseki: The Korean Style
K29: Reducing Territorial Frameworks, by Fujisawa Shuko

The Road Map to Shodan

by Rob van Zeijst and Richard Bozulich

The Road Map to Shodan is a new series of go books whose aim is to provide the novice player with the strategic principles and tactical skills to rise to the level of an expert player (*shodan* or 1-dan).

Strategic knowledge and tactical skills are of equal importance in go. Since brute-force analysis (or reading) is next to impossible in the opening, strategic principles are emphasized. The fastest way to improve one's opening skills is to learn how to build thick positions, then to turn the influence of these positions into territory. This may seem paradoxical to the beginner, as go is a territorial game, but go is also a strategic game and influence is an important concern.

K82: Volume One: **Handicap-Go Strategy and the Sanrensei Opening**
Making the Transition from Handicap to Even Games

The fastest way to improve one's opening skills is to learn how to build thick positions, then to turn the influence of these positions into territory. This may seem paradoxical to the beginner, as go is a territorial game, but go is also a strategic game and influence is an important concern. The study of handicap go is the natural way to learn how to build thick positions, then to turn the influence of these positions into territory. The handicap stones are placed high on the fourth-line star points, so the black player is forced to think globally. Eventually, the novice will find himself playing Black without a handicap. The easiest way to make the transition from handicap games to even games is to adopt the ***Sanrensei Opening***. In this opening, Black occupies three star points on one side of the board, so the basic strategy of playing for influence used in handicap games is the same.

K83: Volume Two: **The Basic Principles of the Opening and the Middle Game**

Go is played on a very large board consisting of 361 playing points. During the opening phase (the fuseki), there will be perhaps 50 to 100 candidates for a plausible move, and for each of these candidate moves the opponent's many possible responses must also be considered, as well as your responses to each of these responses, and so on. Clearly, an exhaustive search is impractical, so the expert go player needs some principles to guide him in finding the best move.

This book presents those basic strategic principles. The 20 principles presented here will lay the foundations for the study of opening theory in general as well as the currently popular opening systems, such as the Sanrensei Opening, Chinese Opening, etc., presented in other volumes of this series.

K84: Volume Three: **The Basics of Life and Death**

Most go players know that the best way to improve one's tactical and reading skills is to solve life-and-death and tesuji problems. Volume Three is intended as a comprehensive book on life and death for beginning players as well as for kyu-level players. Part One of this volume starts out by presenting all the basic eye spaces. It then shows how three basic tesujis (the hane, the placement, and the throw-in) are used to reduce these eye spaces to one eye and kill the groups. The second part is a life-and-death dictionary that presents 177 basic position that regularly arise from josekis or common middle-game skirmishes in the corners and along the sides. If you have diligently studied this book, you will be able to instantly determine the status of these positions when they arise in your games.

K85: Volume 4: **A Survey of the Basic Tesujis**

Volume Four is a concise dictionary of tesuji. It presents all the different tesujis in the order of how commonly they occur. An example of each tesuji is presented followed by six to 12 problems showing the various ways that they can be applied.

Game Collections

K01: Invincible: The Games of Shusaku, edited and compiled by John Power
K07: The 1971 Honinbo Tournament, by Iwamoto Kaoru
K91: Modern Master Games, Vol. 1, The Dawn of Tournament Go
    by Rob van Zeijst and Richard Bozulich
K92: Modern Master Games, Vol. 2, The 2014 Ten-Game Match
    between Gu Li and Lee Sedol, Part One: Games One to Five
    by Rob van Zeijst
K93: Modern Master Games, Vol. 2, The 2014 Ten-Game Match
    between Gu Li and Lee Sedol, Part Two: Games Six to Eight
    by Michael Redmond 9-dan and Rob van Zeijst

Go World

Go World was a quarterly magazine covering the Japanese and international tournament scene. Analysis of games from tournaments and instructional articles for players of all levels. Back issues are still available.

A complete set of Go World from the first issue to the last issue, #129, is available on three DVDs from Kiseido Digital. Go to *http://www.kiseidodigital.com*.

To order books and go equipment, go to the online shop of Kiseido's web site at *http://www.kiseido.com*, or send an email to *kiseido61@yahoo.com*. You can also write direct to Kiseido's main office in Japan as follows:

Kiseido Publishing Company,
Kagawa 4-48-32, Chigasaki-shi
Kanagawa-ken, Japan 253-0082;
Phone /FAX +81-467-81-0605
e-mail: *kiseido@yk.rim.or.jp*; *http://www.kiseido.com*